Contents

**Part Two: Themes and Sample Questions
         & Answers**

Students' Guide
to
Jane Eyre

Joy Rosemary Atfield

First Published in 1992 by
Tynron Press
Unit 3 Turnpike Close
Lutterworth
Leicestershire LE17 4JA
England

ISBN 1-85646-040-1

Typeset by Points Prepress Service Pte Ltd
Printed in Singapore by Lolitho (Pte) Ltd

Introduction

I hope you will enjoy studying this novel. Although it was first published nearly a hundred and fifty years ago, in 1847, it has interested and involved readers ever since. It deals with characters and situations which are still familiar to us now, or which are so vividly described that we can understand and sympathise, 'seeing' them in our mind's eye.

Charlotte Bronte created a character, Jane Eyre, who has appealed to thousands of readers. She is not particularly clever or beautiful, so the ordinary reader can identify with her; yet she has extraordinary qualities of determination and perseverence which the reader can admire. This is one of the great skills of the author throughout the novel, the blending of the ordinary and the extraordinary. The details of people, houses, and landscape are detailed and clear, set firmly in the real world; yet there are also thrilling and sometimes disturbing descriptions of dreams, ghostly figures and mysterious events.

The story follows the development of Jane from a frightened orphan child in the unfriendly home of her aunt and cousins to a mature and perceptive woman in her own home enjoying a mutually satisfying relationship with her husband. The stages of Jane's life are marked by the different places in which she lives; first, at Gateshead; then at school at Lowood; next as a governess at Thornfield; later at Moor House; then in the school house at Morton and eventually at Ferndean with Mr Rochester.

The novel also follows the relationship between Jane and Mr Rochester, but it is not in every way a traditional romantic novel, as Charlotte Bronte deliberately created her central character to be different from the typically beautiful but somewhat empty-headed romantic heroine. She does incorporate many of the elements of the Romantic tradition, however, to very powerful effect. The power of

the special values are important
'head of gods' closed in
Thornfield

the supernatural; parallels between the natural world and the feelings and situations of the characters; the interest she shows in the psychological aspect of human nature; all these show her writing to be in tune with the Romantic movement in literature, developed by poets such as Coleridge and Wordsworth.

If you have not read other novels written in the nineteenth century, you may at first find the language more formal and elaborate than that which you have been used to, but once you are engaged with the characters and events, as I expect you soon will be, you will quickly get used to this. There is a glossary at the end of the guide to explain particular words which you may not have come across, or whose meanings have slightly changed in our time.

It is often interesting to know a little about the life and background of a writer. In the case of Charlotte Bronte, there are some events and situations in her own life which link directly with her novel, and these are worth considering. She was born in 1816, the third child in a family of six children. Her father was a clergyman who had charge of a parish in Haworth, Yorkshire. Her mother died when Charlotte was very young, and when her two elder sisters also died, Charlotte was left in charge of her two younger sisters, Anne and Emily, and her brother, Branwell. Thus, like her character Jane, she was expected to show independence and maturity beyond her years (although there was an aunt who came to take on the role of housekeeper).

She attended a school with her sisters at Cowan Bridge, which was funded by a religious organisation and run by a clergyman on whom Charlotte based Mr Brocklehurst. The descriptions of Lowood school in the novel, and the desperate unhappiness of many of the pupils, sadly reflect what Charlotte herself suffered. It was while attending this school that her older sisters died, and the illness and death of Helen Burns are as much the account of the experience of her elder sister Maria as of a fictional character.

The Bronte children grew up in a fairly isolated community, and their father had all the duties of a parish clergyman to attend to, and could not spare them much time. He did read to them, but from his own books and journals, which he also encouraged them to read for themselves; he involved them in discussions of politics, literature and history; thus they were exposed to much material which was very adult in style and content. This obviously led to quite mature tastes in reading and conversation and led Charlotte to become a very serious child and an avid reader, like her character Jane. The Bronte children made up long, involved stories for their own entertainment, the 'Gondal' sagas, and retreated into the world of imagination, much as Jane did, to escape unhappiness or boredom.

Charlotte had several posts as governess when she left school, but none of these was very successful or pleasant for her. The descriptions of the condescending attitudes of characters in the novel to Jane in her role of governess must have been taken from the writer's own experience. After a time as assistant teacher at a boarding school in Brussels, which Charlotte attended with her sister Emily to learn French and German, the sisters hoped to set up their own school, but when this failed, they decided to try to publish their poems and stories. Charlotte's great interest in education and the most effective way of teaching young children and encouraging their talents is clearly shown in a number of incidents in the novel. The need for publication of her novel and those of her sisters under male pseudonyms shows something of the bigoted and exclusive attitude of the literary world of the time; the 'feminist' perspective which seems to be clear in a variety of authorial comments and reactions of the central character in the novel probably stems from Charlotte's reaction to this.

If you are interested to read more than the very brief details given here, the biographical novel about the Brontes, *Dark Quartet,* by Lynne Reid Banks, published by Penguin books, is well worth reading. If you are using the Penguin edition of *Jane Eyre,* from which the page references in this guide are taken, there is an excellent introduction which you would probably gain most from if you read it *after* you have read the novel as it contains some very interesting critical comments and a little more detail about the life of Charlotte Bronte.

This guide will take you through the novel chapter by chapter, suggesting significant and interesting points about the content and style, with questions to help you reflect on what you have read. Your own response, however, is equally valid. When you have read the novel, there may well be other points of detail you would want to emphasise. A guide will start you on the way to a full appreciation of the text but to answer examination questions effectively, you need to express your own ideas as well. You will find suggestions for preparation and practice of examination questions after the summaries and commentaries.

PART ONE

Chapter Studies

Chapter One

Summary

In the first chapter the titular heroine of the story, Jane Eyre, is introduced. She lives with the Reed family but is seen very much as their inferior, little better than a servant. She is cruelly treated by the 14-year-old son of the household and regarded as a nuisance by the mother. She hides behind a curtain to read on a window seat after being rejected by the family and is wounded when John Reed throws the book she has borrowed at her head, claiming that she has no right to it and that he is soon to be the owner of the house and all the Reed property.

Commentary

Jane's situation in the Reed household is described. The novel opens right "in the middle of things": "we" and "I" are referred to with no explanation, there is a reference to "Mrs Reed", but no explanation of who she is or what her relationship is to the narrator. This means that the reader is on the one hand bewildered, yet also taken immediately into the experience of the characters, as if he or she knows them already. The atmosphere is grim and dark, suggested by the references to "the leafless shrubbery", the "cold winter wind", "sombre clouds" and "penetrating" rain (p.39).

The narrator of the story is clearly in a difficult and unpleasant situation; although relieved at not having to take a walk, the remarks about the usual "saddened" feeling after being told off by the nurse and the insecurity in being "humbled" by a sense of "inferiority" introduce the contrast between the narrator and the other characters mentioned: "Eliza, John and Georgiana Reed" (p.39).

This contrast is emphasised in the next paragraph, where with a slightly envious and sarcastic tone the narrator comments on the comfort and privilege of the other children. They are described as "clustered" around their mother, keeping anyone else out of the comfortable circle; they are "darlings", yet the reference to their normal behaviour, "quarelling" or "crying", implies that this is just an outward appearance to gain their mother's approval at the expense of the narrator. To Mrs Reed, they are "contented, happy little children" (p.39), whereas Jane, now referred to by her name, is seen as awkard and insolent, even though she only asks what she is supposed to have done wrong.

The importance of books as an escape is introduced. Jane seems to have one solace in this unhappy situation, which she finds in books. When she is hidden behind the curtain, sitting on the window seat in the breakfast room, she feels secure and happy, "shrined in double retirement" (p.39), both away from the disagreeable family and the cold wet weather, hidden from the view of anyone entering the room. The power of the description of the weather, from which she is protected by the large window, creates a bleak and desperate mood: the day is "drear"; the rain "ceaseless"; all nature seems drenched and dismal, the lawn "wet", the bushes "storm-beat" (p.40).

The book Jane has taken down from the shelves has illustrations which reflect her isolated and desolate situation, as she looks at pictures of "solitary rocks and promontories", "bleak shores", "forlorn regions of dreary space". Her resilience, to be shown as the novel progresses, is perhaps embodied in the "rock standing up alone in a sea of billow and spray" (p.40).

The impression of an adult reflecting on childhood experience is shown in the authorial comments: the pictures, at the time she was looking at them, are perceived later to have been "mysterious often to my undeveloped understanding and imperfect feelings" (p.41), and the reassurance and security of the knowledge of a fantasy world into which the child can escape through stories is remembered on recollection of "... the tales Bessie sometimes narrated", which "... fed our eager attention with passages of love and adventure ..." (p.41).

Jane's unfair and brutal treatment by John Reed and his partial mother is described. John Reed's interruption of Jane's retreat is aggressive and spiteful; he ridicules her dejected state, nicknaming her "Madam Mope", demeans her by calling her "animal" and later "rat", and ensures she will be reprimanded by his mother for allegedly running "out into the rain" (p.41). His lack of intelligence is shown in his inability to realise where Jane is hiding, as he "was not quick either of vision or conception" (p.41). His imperious nature is shown in his demand that she approach him and his insistence that she address him by his title, "Master Reed", even though at 14 he is only four years older than she.

Mrs Reed's indulgence of her unpleasant son is made clear in the reference to her having kept him away from school and spoiled him by giving him too many cakes and sweets. The repugnance the narrator feels for him is well shown by comments on his "dingy", "flabby" and "sallow" appearance (p.41).

The harsh treatment Jane receives at John's hands is cruel and cowardly, as he takes plans to hide the truth of it from his mother and she would clearly take his part against Jane, being "blind and deaf on the subject" of his bullying (p.42). The cowering despair Jane feels is movingly described, as she refers to her physical recoil, "every morsel of flesh on my bones shrank when he came near" (p.42), and the frequency and continuity of this abuse is made clear by references to her being "habitually obedient", "accustomed" and "dreading" the inevitable blow (p.42). She does have some defence in her ability to detach herself from the situation and consider the "disgusting and ugly appearance" of her assailant, and in her accusation that he is like "a murderer ... slave driver ... the Roman emperors" (p.43).

The severity of the cut Jane receives on her head is dismissed in comparison with the concern of nurse, maid and children's mother for John, immediately assuming he is the one who has been attacked: "Dear! dear! What a fury to fly at Master John!" (p.43). This unfair and unjustified reaction is compounded in the ominous last sentence of the chapter as Jane is "borne upstairs" to be locked in the red-room as punishment (p.43).

Questions on Chapter One

1. How does the description of the weather and atmosphere reflect Jane's feelings in this chapter?
2. What impression do you gain of the personality of Mrs Reed?
3. What differences do you find between the treatment of Jane and the other children?

Glossary

P.39   Sombre: dark and gloomy
P.41   Mope: to be sad and listless
P.42: Habitually: normally, usually

Chapter Two

Summary

Jane is imprisoned in the red-room, a bedroom formerly used by Mrs Reed's late husband, where he died and from which his body was taken for burial. Jane is brutally pushed into the room by the nurse Bessie and maid Abbot, and made to sit still until dark. Jane considers the injustice of the treatment she receives from the family and servants and this leads to a frightening hallucination which so disturbs her that she screams out and the servants and Mrs Reed come running. She is harshly considered to be merely drawing attention to herself and is once more imprisoned in the room, where she is so distressed that she has a fit and falls unconscious.

Commentary

Jane's punishment; a description of the red-room and her feelings. Jane's struggle in the arms of the nurse and her maid is vividly described; the narrator recalls how she becomes almost deranged in her resistance, "I was a trifle beside myself; or rather *out* of myself"; the aggressive treatment she receives is clearly shown as she is "thrust" on a stool, "arrested" by the others' hands and threatened with bondage (p.44). The cruelty she suffers is not only physical, but mental. Charlotte Bronte makes a departure from other novels written at the time of *Jane Eyre,* when she showed the psychological effects of childhood experiences on the adult. Jane is also threatened by the wrath of God, and with the horrible uncertainty of "something bad" which "might be permitted to come down the chimney and fetch you away" (p.45).

The constant reference to Jane's dependence on the 'charity' of the Reed family is made clear when the silent response to the nurse's reminder of her obligation is shown to be partly because these words "were not new"; she has been reminded of her inequality with the Reed children for as long as she can remember: "my very first recollections of existence included hints of the same kind" (p.45).

The description of the red-room, in which Jane is locked up, is very elaborate and detailed. The impressive and formal nature of the furniture and fabrics is emphasised by comments describing the bed as a "tabernacle", and the chair as a "throne" (p.45). It is indeed a kind of shrine, as the reader learns it was where Mr Reed died and it has been kept intact since. Thus the atmosphere in the room is cold and remote, it is "lonely" and "guarded from frequent intrusion" (p.45). The moving description of Jane's sense of injustice and bewilderment is skilfully related to the reflection of the young, vulnerable girl in the mirror, "the strange little figure" with "glittering eyes ... moving where all else was still ... (p. 46).

Jane's reflections on the Reed family and her treatment by them. Further details of John Reed's behaviour establish him as a thoroughly selfish and destructive character, who gains pleasure from others' discomfort and suffering. He "killed the little pea-chicks, set the dogs at the sheep, stripped the hothouse vines of their fruit ..." (p.47). Yet despite this wanton cruelty and his insolence towards his mother, he is spoiled and petted and Jane is rejected. Her thoughts about this situation are shown to overwhelm her as she struggles to comprehend the injustice: "What a consternation of soul was mine that dreary afternoon! How all my brain was in tumult, and all my heart in insurrection!" (p.47).

The narrative technique of the adult looking back at the child's situation is again used to comment on the realisation that Jane is so different in character and outlook to the Reed family that she will probably never be accepted. She feels that had she been livelier, more vital and active, even more demanding, a "careless, exacting, handsome, romping child" (p.47), Mrs Reed, her children and the servants would have been more positive in their treatment of her.

The psychological effects of Jane's imprisonment are effectively shown as the light fades and her thoughts become morbid and even suicidal, as she thinks of starving herself to death and dwells on the knowledge of Mr Reed, her uncle, being entombed in the vault of the church. The reader is given a little more background information about Jane's situation as it is revealed that it was Mr Reed who had initially introduced her into the household, and that Mrs Reed has the imposition of responsibility for her as a legacy after her husband's death. Again the adult voice of Jane considers this situation with the objectivity which she could not have been expected to have at ten years old: "It must have been most irksome to find herself bound by a hard-wrung pledge to stand in the stead of a parent to a strange child she could not love ..." (p.48).

Jane's fear and dread turn into a supernatural hallucination.

Jane's superstition takes hold of her as she thinks of her dead uncle and the possibility of his ghost walking, disturbed by the treatment she has received. The oppressive hallucinations of this nightmarish idea are vividly conveyed, in both mental and physical terms, "prepared as my mind was for horror, shaken as my nerves were by agitation ... My heart beat thick, my head grew hot; a sound filled my ears..." (p.49). The mounting fears of the child are described as culminating in a terrified sense of claustrophobia: Jane feels "suffocated" and she shakes the lock, but inevitably the reaction of her oppressors is not sympathetic; the insensitivity of Abbot is shown clearly when she dismisses Jane's intense distress as merely "naughty tricks" (p.49).

Again in these descriptions the adult narrator reflects on the incident, commenting that the true source of the light in the room which so terrified her was probably "a gleam from a lantern carried by someone across the lawn" (p.49), and that Mrs Reed's harsh reaction of insisting that she stay in the room another hour was because "she sincerely looked on me as a compound of virulent passions, mean spirit, and dangerous duplicity" (p.50). The end of the chapter is dramatic as the author recalls the fit and subsequent faint she suffered, and "unconsciousness closed the scene" (p.50).

Questions on Chapter Two

1. What is the red-room like and how does Jane feel when she is locked in?
2. Which further members of the Reed household are introduced in this chapter, and what kind of personalities do they have?
3. What are the differences between Mrs Reed and her former husband in their attitude to Jane?
4. How does the author show herself to be an adult writing about her childhood experiences?

Glossary

P.45 Tabernacle: sanctuary, temple, place of worship
P.47 Romping: lively, overactive, boisterous
P.50 Virulent: bitter, infectious, poisonous

Chapter Three

Summary

Jane is cared for in the nursery after her fit in the red-room, and the doctor is called to attend her. Bessie attempts to cheer her up by offering her various treats, but Jane is so consumed with despair and the after-effects of shock that she can take no pleasure in these. After a conversation with the doctor, the suggestion is made that Jane should go away to school, and Mrs Reed readily agrees as this will relieve her of the responsibility of Jane's care.

Commentary

Jane recovers after the fit brought on by shock when she was locked up. The gradual awakening of Jane in the nursery is very well described, with the description of things distorted at first until she becomes accustomed to her surroundings. As she comes to consciousness, the nurse and doctor's voices are "hollow" and "muffled"; the "terrible red glare, crossed with thick black bars" becomes "the nursery fire". The normal deprivation of her life with the Reeds is emphasised by the suggestion that it is unusual for her to experience any gentleness, as she is supported "more tenderly than I had ever been raised or upheld before" (p.51).

Jane's sense of relief when she realises that there is someone with her who is not part of the Gateshead household shows how disturbed she has become in her constant fear and insecurity; she feels "so sheltered and befriended" when the doctor is beside her, but "as he closed the door after him, all the room darkened and my heart again sank: inexpressible sadness weighed it down" (p.51). The use of light and darkness to contrast happier and sadder moods is conventional, but Charlotte Bronte adds to this by emphasising how difficult Jane finds it to verbalise her wretched state: the sadness is "inexpressible"; she has been so damaged by the effects of the Reeds' cruelty, her sensitivity has led to depression so deep that not even the things she would normally take delight in can rouse her.

Bessie's offers of treats and attempts to cheer Jane only lead to further suffering. This lack of interest is shown clearly when ironically Bessie tries to encourage Jane with offers of food and drink, which she recognises sarcastically as "wonderful civility" (p.52). A sinister note is suggested in the whisperings of the nurse and maid after they think Jane has fallen asleep, with vague references to ghostly presences, sights and sounds all contributing to a very eerie atmosphere: "Something passed her, all dressed in white ... great black dog ... light in the churchyard ..." (p.52). Inevitably this leads to Jane's continuing terror, enveloped in a terrible dread of something unknown yet fearsome, and "the watches of that long night passed in ghastly wakefulness" (p.52). There is a dramatically direct comment on Mrs Reed's responsibilities in this situation which shows the narrator to be influenced even in adulthood by the trauma of her early years: "Yes, Mrs Reed, to you I owe some fearful pangs of mental suffering". Her response is biblical, connecting her innocent sufferings with those of Christ, as she continues, "I ought to forgive you, for you knew not what you did ..." (p.52).

The continuation of Jane's silent suffering and depression is shown in the way that previously admired and pleasurable objects are affected by her generally gloomy perception. The beautifully decorated plate which she had so often longed to hold "seemed strangely faded" (p.53), and the book of the story of *Gulliver's Travels* also failed to please her, and seemed "eerie and dreary", like the physical situation she was in. This psychological state is examined most sensitively by the author, showing an understanding well ahead of her time. The fact that Jane cannot eat the tart she is offered is another aspect of this depressive state, explained as "coming, like most favours long deferred and often wished for, too late!" (p.53).

The doctor does not really understand Jane's misery, but suggests the idea of Jane going to school. The "doleful" ballad Bessie sings only serves to intensify Jane's misery, and when the doctor enquires about the cause of her unhappiness, his lack of real understanding is clear as he tries to determine the reason, and seems to accept Bessie's suggestions rather than really listening to Jane herself. When he talks to her alone, though, he shows that he realises that there is more to the problem than mere "pettishness", but again he does not really attempt to understand the underlying cause, dismissively suggesting "you are a baby after all! You are afraid of ghosts?" (p.55). Jane's staunch defence of her reaction to the imprisonment in the red-room shows her resilience and self-respect, still intact despite her negative mood, as she retorts, "Neither Bessie nor anyone else will go into it at night, if they can help it; and it was cruel to shut me up alone without a candle" (p.55).

The narrator's adult comment emphasises the extreme difficulty Jane has in expressing her reasons for unhappiness: "Children can feel, but they cannot analyse their feelings" (p.56), and in the conversation with the doctor some further background to Jane's solution is given, that she is orphaned and does not know of any other relatives. If she does have any, they are, according to Mrs Reed, likely to be poor, and Jane has clearly been influenced by the Reeds' superior and negative attitude to those less fortunate than themselves, giving her the impression of "ragged clothes, scanty food, fireless grates, rude manners, and debasing vices" (p.56).

The doctor's mention of school also produces stereotyped images in Jane's mind, as she admits, "I scarcely knew what school was", yet she ominously skates over the references she has heard from Bessie of "appalling" accounts of the discipline meted out in schools she has heard of, and concentrates her ideas on the more positive "accomplishments attained by these same young ladies" (p.57). This is to prove ironic later as Jane discovers even more deprived conditions once she herself gets to school.

Mrs Reed eagerly accepts the doctor's advice, and unwittingly Jane has consigned herself to a future more bleak than the experiences she has already endured. The impression is given of Jane being regarded as almost inanimate, as she is not consulted at all about her future; she gains her information through overhearing the conversations of Bessie and Abbot, "when both sat sewing in the nursery one night" (p.58). At the end of the chapter the information is given, again gleaned by Jane only by listening to others, that her parents died of typhoid. The continuance of her inferiority complex is ensured when the conversation continues with suggestion that if she were a more engaging child her situation might attract far more sympathy: "if she were a nice, pretty child, one might compassionate her forlornness ..." (p.58). The final comments about food show the lack of real concern for Jane, and emphasise the comparative freedom of the servants, able to eat as they please.

Questions on Chapter Three

1. How is Jane's return to consciousness described?
2. What attempts does Bessie make to encourage Jane and how does Jane react?
3. What impression do you gain of the doctor?
4. What is important about the suggestion the doctor makes to Mrs Reed?
5. What further details of Jane's personality and background do you gain through this chapter?

Glossary

P.53 Deferred: put off, denied
P.55 Pettishness: petulance, sullenness
P.56 Analyse: examine in detail
P.57 Accomplishments: achievements, skills
P.58 Compassionate: sympathise with, pity

Chapter Four

Summary

Time drags for Jane as she awaits the change of going to school. She meets the formidable headmaster, Mr Brocklehurst, and is accused of deceitfulness, in his presence, by Mrs Reed. When he has left, Jane violently accuses Mrs Reed of neglect and harsh treatment, and insists she is the deceitful one. This outburst reinforces Mrs Reed's determination to send Jane to school as soon as possible.

Commentary

The contrast of Jane's life to that of the Reed children is emphasised.

Jane looks forward to the possibility of a change in her circumstances and environment once she is well again, but nothing is said about her going to school for some time. There is a realistic description of the way that time seems to drag for Jane: the change "tarried"; she "brooded" over the possibility of going away, always awaiting some remark from Mrs Reed (p.59). She is even more isolated than before; the suggestion is that she is regarded as almost another species than the Reed children; Mrs Reed "had drawn a more marked line of separation" (p.59) between them and Jane. The children are told to keep away, and even the favourite, John, is reprimanded for going near her when he starts another story of her attacking him, despite it being in self-defence, "roused by the same sentiment of deep ire and desperate revolt which had stirred my corruption before" (p.59).

Jane's sense of outraged justice leads to her protest that the Reed children "are not fit to associate with me" (p.59) rather than the other way round, and her resistance and resilience are again displayed in her challenge after Mrs Reed has knocked her down: "What would Uncle Reed say to you, if he were alive?" (p.60). As usual this resistance is met with physical abuse — Jane's ears are boxed and she is shaken "most soundly". The confusion and hurt repressed in the child are clearly shown when she begins to question her own sense of righteousness, half-believing the accusations made of her: "for I felt, indeed, only bad feelings surging in my breast" (p.60). This description of the physical effects of emotion make the character's feelings easy to understand and identify with.

Jane's pitiful isolation from the normal and celebratory events of family life is made clear, when in the description of the Reeds' Christmas Charlotte Bronte emphasises the way that Jane only sees and hears small glimpses of the activities in the house, while she is left up in the nursery. Her only awareness of the "gaiety" is when she watches "the daily apparelling of Eliza and Georgiana" and listens to the various sounds which float up to her, such as "the sound of the piano or the harp ... the jingling of glass and china ... the broken hum of conversation ..." (p.60). Even Bessie deserts Jane, as she "used to take herself off to the lively regions of the kitchen ... generally bearing the candle along with her" (p.60).

Jane's lack of comfort and security in the Reed household is made clear. Jane's situation is made even more poignant as she is left alone in the dark and hides herself away in her bed with only an old doll for company. Once again the adult voice of the narrator recalls this in her own past, and comments on the extraordinary importance a very shabby old toy can have in such circumstances: "It puzzles me now to remember with what absurd sincerity I doted on this little toy, half fancying it alive and capable of sensation" (p.61). This situation is clearly an example of projection; the child is projecting on to the doll the responsiveness she wishes she could find in other people; she needs the doll as a substitute for real human love. The narrator further comments in this regard: "human beings must love something, and, in the dearth of worthier objects of affection, I contrived to find a pleasure in loving and cherishing a faded graven image ... (p.61).

The author gives the reader some more detail of the nurse Bessie, commenting on the occasional kindnesses she gives Jane, tucking her into bed and kissing her goodnight and, as usual with hindsight, suggests she must have been lively and intelligent, as "she was smart in all she did, and had a remarkable knack of narrative" (p.61). Despite her pleasant appearance, "with black hair, dark eyes, very nice features", she was nevertheless moody and could be cruel as she "had a capricious and hasty temper, and indifferent ideas of principle or justice" (p.61).

Jane's experience of the first meeting with the headmaster, Mr Brocklehurst, is described in detail. The precise details given of the day on which Jane does hear more about going to school emphasise its importance long before the meeting with Mr Brocklehurst is described. The date and time are mentioned, the details of others' activities, such as Eliza "putting on her bonnet and warm garden-coat to go and feed her poultry" (p.61) and Georgiana "interweaving her curls with artificial flowers" (p.62), and eventually the sight of the carriage being driven through the gates and the ringing of the door bell are all mentioned without any indication at first who the visitor is, as the reader is then in the same situation as the character. Jane, in fact, is quickly distracted by "the spectacle of a little hungry robin" (p.62), and unaware of the importance of the visitor and how he will influence her future.

The rush of preparations performed by Bessie in order to make Jane presentable for the visitor increases the pace of the story: Bessie comes "running upstairs", is "in too great a hurry to listen", and "then hurrying me to the top of the stairs, bid me go down directly" (p.63). The agitation of the nurse affects Jane who becomes nervous and uncertain; when she reaches the breakfast-room door she is "intimidated and trembling", and just stood there for "ten minutes in agitated hesitation" (p.63). Suspense is increased as Jane wonders what or who she will see on the other side of the door, and the situation is almost amusing as she faces what appears to be to her "a black pillar!" (p.63). This first impression of Mr Brocklehurst is most appropriate, as he turns out to be almost inhuman, more like a stone pillar than a man, showing little emotion, as if he does not have ordinary human feelings; his face is "grim" and "like a carved mask" (p.63).

The fearsome nature of the man is clearly shown in the first exchange between him and Jane; at first he talks about her rather than to her: "Her size is small; what is her age?" and there is no attempt made to put her at her ease. His question "are you a good child?" (p.64) is, for a child as scrupulous and honest as Jane, impossible to answer "in the affirmative", as Jane has been told repeatedly that she is not good; even if she still believes herself to be good she could not say that she was. Mrs Reed, of course, suggests she is not at all good. Mr Brocklehurst continues to appear menacing and frightening to the little girl before him; when he bends down to talk to her, Jane is amazed at "what a face he had ... what a great nose! and what a mouth! and what large, prominent teeth! (p.64). The description is reminiscent of the description of the wolf in the fairy tale of *Little Red Riding Hood,* who was pretending to be a kind grandmother and really intended to eat up the little girl in that story. Jane probably fears something similar as she has a vivid imagination.

Jane's truthful nature is tested and she is disconcerted by the aggressive attitude of Mr Brocklehurst. Jane's practical nature is stressed in her response to the question she is asked about going to hell: she suggests the best way to avoid this is to "keep in good health and not die" (p.64), which might well have sounded impertinent to adult ears. Mr Brocklehurst's reply to this is morbid and sinister: "How can you keep in good health? Children younger than you die daily ..." (p.64). As the conversation continues, he is referred to as "my interrogator" (p.65), and certainly the exchange is very formal and harsh.

There is an example of the narrator's ironic humour in her description of Mr Brocklehurst's reference to the little boy who always asked to learn a psalm rather than have a ginger nut - obviously he had realised that he got a reward if he said this, and consequently ensured that he received two gingernuts! The lack of understanding of children's perceptions is clear in the comments Mr Brocklehurst makes about God changing Jane's heart, as she takes his words literally, intending to ask a question about "the manner in which the operation of changing my heart was to be performed" (p.65).

The foreboding already established about Jane's future at school is extended when Mrs Reed insists that "teachers were requested to keep a strict eye on her" and emphasises what she sees as "a tendency to deceit" (p.65), which is really only Jane's understandable reserve in the unpleasant atmosphere in which she has been brought up. Jane begins to realise that such comments will inevitably lead to a difficult time for her later: "I dimly perceived that she was already obliterating hope from the new phase of existence which she destined me to enter" (p.66).

Mr Brocklehurst uses dreadful images of destruction and suffering to threaten Jane: "... all liars will have their portion in the lake burning with fire and brimstone" (p.66), and the deprivation of the girls which Jane will soon join is made clear in the reference to their looking "quiet and plain", and as if "they had never seen a silk gown before" (p.66), when Augusta Brocklehurst visited the school with her mother. It is this bleak prospect of rigid authority, threatening punishment and inhuman "system" into which Jane is to be thrust, and the imprisonment is to be total, as Mrs Reed clearly wants to be totally rid of any personal responsibility for the child in future. She asks that "as for the vacations she will, with your permission, spend them always at Lowood" (p.66).

The irony of the narrator's viewpoint is shown again as she records the comment of the despicably smug Mr Brocklehurst as he speaks of the school and the girls as " ... that nursery of chosen plants" (p.67), whereas when Jane gets there she quickly realises that no plant, let alone a young girl, could flourish in the bleak and desolate atmosphere. As the headmaster leaves, he yet again shows the rigid and punitive approach he takes towards his charges as he leaves Jane with a book of cautionary tales, describing terrible fates of children who have broken rules of behaviour, such as "the awfully sudden death of Martha G" (p.67).

Jane's relationship with Mrs Reed deteriorates even further as she challenges her about the treatment she has received. It is only at this stage of the novel that the reader is given a description of Mrs Reed, probably because Jane is so glad, at the time, to be leaving her, and takes in every detail of her appearance: "... square-shouldered and strong limbed ... a somewhat large face ... her brow was low, her chin large and prominent ..." (p.67). The description suggests that she was probably very well satisfied with her life, "illness never came near her; she was an exact and clever manager, her household and tenantry were thoroughly under her control" - possibly she was unaware of the damage she was doing to the young Jane; she had no conception of Jane as even of the same kind as her children, and as a widow in good circumstances she had more advantages and freedoms than most women in the society in which she live.

The realism of the writing in this chapter is emphasised when Jane's natural resentment and sense of injustice surface in her denunciation of Mrs Reed. Jane would have been too good to be true if she had not retaliated after the awful experience of her unfair presentation to Mr Brocklehurst. The physical manifestation of emotional feeling is again clearly expressed, as "a passion of resentment fomented now within me ..." and "I gathered my energies and launched them in this blunt sentence ..." (p.68). The challenge to her aunt rises to a climax of a child's hatred and sense of oppression: "... if anyone asks me how I liked you, and how you treated me, I will say the very thought of you makes me sick, and that you treated me with miserable cruelty" (p.68). The final outburst culminates with the accusation made against Jane, but turned now on the true deserver: "You are deceitful!" (p.69).

The idea of the novel as a charting of the progress of the developing independence and forming of character of the heroine is shown in the description of Jane's reaction to her condemnation of her aunt. "It seemed as if an invisible bond had burst, and that I had struggled out into unhoped-for liberty ... It was the hardest battle I had fought and the first victory I had gained" (p.69). The images of strife, "bond ... burst ... struggled ... battle", emphasise the continued struggle Jane will have through life to establish and defend her individuality. Mrs Reed's reaction is almost comic in its hypocrisy: "she was ... rocking herself to and fro"; "Is there anything else you wish for, Jane?"; "now return to the nursery — there's a dear ..." (p.69). She has quite clearly been astonished and disturbed at the intensity of Jane's feeling and her attempts to pacify her are shown to be ridiculous and somewhat pathetic through the change of tone to a pleading false sympathy.

The adult authorial comment is used again to reflect on the inevitable counter-reaction of Jane's realisation of what she has done: "A child cannot quarrel with its elders, as I had done ... without experiencing afterwards the pang of remorse and the chill of reaction" (p.69). A most vivid and effective image is used, consistent with the images of strife earlier, of a battle-scarred landscape: "... the same ridge, black and blasted after the flames are dead, would have represented as meetly my subsequent condition" (p.69). The alliteration of "black" and "blasted" reinforces the dull and bleak sense of "the dreariness of my hated and hating position" (p.70). A further image conveying this reaction links with the physical manifestation illustrated previously, as the contrasting feelings of triumph and dread associated with vengeance are described in terms of taste: "an aromatic wine it seemed, on swallowing, warm and racy; its after-flavour, metallic and corroding ..." (p.70).

The usual reassurance brought by the pleasure of reading cannot be found by Jane in her distressed mood; the escapism of "some Arabian tales" fails to fascinate her as it had previously done. By this means the author shows how disturbed she was, and the scenery and weather reflect this bleak state as they did at the opening of the novel: "... the black frost reigned ... leaves ... stiffened together ... the short grass was nipped and blanched" (p.70). Bessie's call breaks into Jane's depressed state, and she "seemed cheerful, even though, as usual, she was somewhat cross" (p.70). The liveliness of the maid breaches the terrible sense of alienation caused by Jane's outburst, and even though she is irritated, Bessie represents some kind of human comfort for Jane, who reacts by putting "my two arms around her", an action "more frank and fearless than any I was habituated to indulge in" (p.71). This once again emphasises the normal lack of warmth and friendliness Jane suffers in the Reed household.

The conflicting reactions of Bessie to Jane's situation must also add to her confusion and uncertainty, as at one point she recommends, "You should be bolder" (p.71) and later when Jane does show some spirit, she refers to her as a "little sharp thing", and demands, "What makes you so venturesome and hardy?" (p.71). She offers the treat of tea with her and cake to eat, but Jane is unimpressed, as this is all part of the preparations for her removal to school, which although she has longed for, will probably hold, Jane realises, as many terrors and discomforts as she has already known, in a different environment: "I shall soon have another set of people to dread" (p.71). Bessie is clearly disconcerted by the containment and restraint of her charge, yet seemingly unaware of her own part in causing Jane to react in this way: "How coolly my little lady says it! I dare say if I were to ask you for a kiss you wouldn't give it me: you'd say you'd *rather* not" (p.72). The final image of the chapter is one of warmth and comfort, but the wry comment, "Even for me life had its gleams of sunshine" (p.72), emphasises that this happy scene is seen in retrospect, after many harder and more unpleasant experiences have been endured.

Questions on Chapter Four

1. How does the author suggest that time drags for Jane as she expects to go away to school?
2. How are the differences between Jane's lifestyle and that of the Reed children made clear?
3. What is your impression of Mr Brocklehurst in this chapter?
4. What indications do you gain from this chapter that school will not be a happy experience for Jane?
5. What finally makes Jane stand up to Mrs Reed, and how does she express her feelings?
6. How does (a) Jane (b) Mrs Reed (c) Bessie react to Jane's boldness?

Glossary

P.59   Tarried: went slowly, held back
P.59   Brooded: thought deeply
P.59   Ire: anger
P.60   Aparelling: dressing
P.61   Sensation: feeling
P.61   Capricious: moody
P.61   Indifferent: poor, careless
P.63   Intimidated: frightened

P.64 Affirmative: positive, agreement
P.66 Perceived: realised
P.66 Obliterating: removing, blotting out
P.69 Pang: sharp pain
P.70 Aromatic: scented
P.70 Racy: exciting, lively
P.71 Habituated: used
P.71 Venturesome: adventurous, daring

Chapter Five

Summary

Jane travels from Gateshead to Lowood School, learns her way about and makes contact with another pupil who will later be named as Helen Burns. Jane's first day at the school is described, with the routines and style of lessons and activities clearly detailed.

Commentary

Jane's farewell to Bessie and Gateshead, and her journey to school are described. The last few hours of Jane's stay in the Reed household are described in a detailed and realistic manner. The early morning start, the moonlit dressing, and Bessie's attempts to encourage Jane to eat something, which she cannot do due to her anticipation of her journey, are easy to picture. The determination of Jane's rejection of Mrs Reed, and her constancy, are shown in the recounting of her final encounter with her aunt, as she tells Bessie, "I covered my face with the bedclothes, and turned from her to the wall" (p.73).

The weather as usual adds to the atmosphere of the situation; the author records that the winter morning was "raw and chill" (p.73), and this discomfort creates a sense of foreboding, suggesting that the next stage of Jane's journey in life will not be comfortable nor very happy. The porter's wife's disapproving attitude to Jane's unaccompanied journey shows how little true sensitivity Mrs Reed has towards her charge, as she is happy to send her on a 50-mile journey "to unknown and ... remote and mysterious regions" (p.74) without the reassurance of a familiar companion.

The details of the journey are vague, to add to the sense of strangeness and uncertainty Jane feels, and her imaginative nature is made clear as she fears "kidnappers, their exploits having frequently figured in Bessie's fireside chronicles" (p.74). Again the weather adds to the gloom and fearfulness of the experience: "I heard a wild wind rushing amongst trees" (p.74), and once she arrives at her destination, "Rain, wind and darkness filled the air" (p.75).

Jane's arrival at the school, her first meeting with Miss Temple and Miss Miller, and first impressions of the school are described. Similar to the meeting with Mr Brocklehurst, the first encounter with the teachers of Lowood School is as if Jane were not there; she is spoken about before she is spoken to: "The child is very young to be sent alone ... She had better be put to bed soon" (p.75). At least the woman she first meets "touched my cheek gently", implying some kindly feeling towards her. The first impression of the school is that of some strange maze: "I passed from compartment to compartment, from passage to passage" (p.76), and the uncertainty and bewilderment this creates in Jane is emphasised further when she eventually sees the other pupils: "their number to me appeared countless" (p.76).

The firm discipline of the school is clear from the first, as orders are called out and girls immediately pack away books and bring supper trays. As before throughout the day, Jane cannot eat when she is offered food, and this adds to the weakness and weariness she feels so that when she eventually gets to bed, "I scarcely noticed what sort of a place the bedroom was" (p.76). The meagre and spartan facilities of the school are shown as Jane has to share a bed; the next morning there is only one basin for six girls to wash in; the school room is "cold and dimly-lit" (p.77). The rigid insistence of Mr Brocklehurst on Bible reading is recalled as the girls have to listen to "a protracted reading of chapters in the Bible" (p.77), before they can have breakfast. The disgusting nature of the burnt porridge the girls are served is very powerfully described: "a nauseous mess — burnt porridge is almost as bad as rotten potatoes" (p.78); the disappointment Jane and the others feel is summed up very effectively in a short sentence: "Breakfast was over, and none had breakfasted" (p.78). The lack of comfort is extended still further in the unattracative uniform the girls have to wear: "it suited them ill, and gave an air of oddity event to the prettiest" (p.79). Even the teachers seem to have been affected by the harshness of the regime at the school, as Jane looks them over they seem "coarse ... fierce ... harsh", and even the more kindly Miss Miller "looked purple, weather-beaten and overworked" (p.79).

The description of Maria Temple, the superintendent of Lowood School, is very precise, and written just as Jane would have taken in the details as she looked at the woman. First a general sense of her appearance, "tall, fair and shapely", the smaller details of her "brown eyes" with "long lashes", her "very dark brown" hair, and then her clothes and accessories, "purple cloth, relieved by a sort of Spanish trimming ... a gold watch shone at her girdle" (p.79-80). The power and presence of this woman is very effectively suggested as when she enters the schoolroom, "the whole school rose simultaneously, as if moved by a common spring" (p.79), and when she speaks, "The tumult ... sank at her voice" (p.80). The implication that Miss Temple is of a more kindly disposition than the headmaster is given through the surprised response to her decision to give the girls bread and cheese for lunch as they could not eat the breakfast. She even seems to feel that explanation is necessary: "It is to be done on my responsibility" (p.80).

More negative hints about the bleakness and lack of comfort in the school life are given. A hint of the damage that the harshness of school life can inflict is given by the reference to "a hollow cough" (p.81), which Jane frequently hears amongst the less hardy girls when they are sent out into the garden despite the "drizzling yellow fog" (p.80). A further sinister note is conveyed by Jane's noticing the word "institution" above the door of the school, suggesting it is more of a prison or workhouse than a place which would encourage the development and education of the girls. The lessons are very much instruction rather than exploration of the subjects studied.

Jane's meeting with Helen Burns, though she does not at first learn her name, shows immediately that Helen is a studious and self-contained girl, as she is reading *Rasselas*, a serious philosophical work which warns against the dangers of false hopes and an over-optimistic view of life. Such a book does not seem to Jane to offer the escapism and fantasy which she has enjoyed in stories to take her mind off her difficulties: "no bright variety seemed spread over the closely-printed pages" (p.82). It is through her conversation with Helen that the earlier fears about the school are confirmed, as Helen's reference to it as "a charity-school" (p.82) and the explanation of the subscription system, make it clear that nothing but the basic necessities will be provided for the girls, and they will be expected to be grateful for the food and clothes provided, even if they are unattractive and insufficient. This is confirmed by the unpleasant description of the dinner served, "redolent of rancid fat ... indifferent potatoes and strange shreds of rusty meat" (p.83).

Helen's comment about Mr Brocklehurst is significantly guarded; she says he "is said to do a great deal of good" (p.83), implying that she herself has had no experience of this benevolent side of the man's character. Jane, and thus the reader, learns more about the other staff of the school, and her own view of the superiority of Miss Temple is confirmed: "she is above the rest" (p.83). The inappropriate treatment of the girls is also suggested through the description of the rest of Jane's first day. Helen is punished by ridicule, having to stand up in the middle of the room for all to stare at her, yet clearly this kind of approach only breeds resentment and hatred in the pupils; Jane notices that "she neither wept nor blushed" but seemed to have mentally retreated "beyond her situation" (p.84).

Questions on Chapter Five

1. What is Jane's journey like, as she travels from one stage of her life to another?
2. What impression of Lowood School do you gain from this chapter?
3. What kind of person do you find (a) Miss Temple (b) Helen Burns (c) Miss Miller to be, as shown in this chapter?
4. What is the significance of Lowood being called an "institution"?

Glossary

P.74   Chronicles: stories
P.79   Simultaneously: at once, all together
P.80   Tumult: disturbance, uproar
P.83   Redolent: smelling
P.83   Rancid: rank, sour, stale

Chapter Six

Summary

Jane continues to find the regime at Lowood harsh and uncomfortable, and is distressed to see the girl she has started to befriend cruelly beaten during a lesson. She develops her relationship with Helen, learns a little more about her background, and is surprised by her saintly and meek acceptance of her treatment.

Commentary

Further description of the girls' way of life at Lowood. The deprivation of the schoolgirls is made clear in this chapter by the description of the intense cold which causes the water to freeze, the tiny portions served at breakfast and the dullness of the lessons, "long and difficult" and expected to be learned "by heart" (p.85). The sympathy of the heroine is directed at Helen Burns, a girl who seems to be mercilessly picked on by the harsh teacher, Miss Scatcherd. Her very name sounds harsh, suggesting a combination of 'scratch' and 'hard', emphasising her cruelty which is shown as she later beats Helen for a small mistake. The use of the girls' surnames also emphasises the impersonal and unfriendly atmostphere of the school.

Jane's attention is wide-ranging as she takes in all around her, yet she seems apart from it in a sense, describing herself as an "actor", having previously been a "spectator" (p.85). This detachment is broken by her distress at the cruel treatment of Helen and her resignation, "my fingers quivered at this spectacle with a sentiment of unavailing and impotent anger ..." (p.86). Jane's frustration at being unable to do anything recalls her feelings at the Reeds' house;

she recognises injustice, yet has no power to alter the situation. Jane's emotional nature is also shown in her reaction to the wild weather outside the school: "I derived from both a strange excitement, and, reckless and feverish, I wished the wind to howl more wildly, the gloom to deepen to darkness ..." (p.87).

Jane learns of Helen's saintly behaviour and Christian commitment. When Jane goes over to talk to Helen later in the day, the power of books to absorb and protect the reader is again shown, as in the first chapter. Helen is completely absorbed, and thus unaffected by her external situation, "silent, abstracted from all around her by the companionship of a book" (p.87). Helen's nature is shown to be far more subdued and resigned than Jane's; she accepts her situation, unpleasant though it may be: "I was sent to Lowood to get an education; and it would be of no use going away until I have attained that object" (p.87). She seems almost too good to be true: her replies to Jane's resentful questions about her treatment are very formal in their language, as if they have been learned by heart along with her schoolwork: "It is far better to endure patiently a smart which nobody feels but yourself, than to commit a hasty action whose evil consequences will extend to all connected with you" (p.88). She is literally living out the biblical instruction to turn the other cheek, and sees the situation from the teacher's point of view: "This is all very provoking to Miss Scatcherd, who is naturally neat, punctual and particular" (p.88).

This reference to Miss Scatcherd provokes a comparison from Jane, and the two teachers are contrasted directly in their methods, Miss Temple teaching by encouragement and concern, totally opposite to Miss Scatcherd's rule of harshness and accusation: "she sees my errors, and tells me of them gently; and, if I do anything worthy of praise, she gives me my meed liberally" (p.88). The whole theme of education is developed in this chapter; the author, through her characters, emphasises how much more satisfying and satisfactory it is to learn through interest and personal involvement than by rote in a harshly disciplined fashion. This is shown in Helen's reply to Jane's observation that she seemed to take in the afternoon's lesson so much better than the way she has described herself normally reacting: "... the subject on which we had been reading had interested me ... I like Charles — I respect him — I pity him, poor murdered king!" (p.89).

Helen's Christian principles are explored in her meek and almost martyred acceptance of her situation; a powerful contrast is shown between Jane's passionate, natural response: "I must dislike those who, whatever I do to please them, persist in disliking me" (p.90) and Helen's controlled, ordered reaction: "It is not violence that best overcomes hate — nor vengeance that most certainly heals injury ... Read the New Testament, and observe what Christ says, and how He acts ..." (p.90). Helen looks beyond the difficulties of her present life, which Jane cannot yet do, and imagines "eternity a rest — a mighty home — not a terror and an abyss ... I live in calm, looking to the end" (p.91). This is extremely mature talk from a young girl, and possibly reflects Christian teaching the author herself heard, but, like Jane, found difficult to accept. The adult sense of endurance in Helen suggests she has never been allowed the free irresponsibility of childhood, but has had to grow up too soon, to find the world a test of the spirit through physical hardship. This attitude is immediately illustrated by action, as she responds to the monitor's interruption of her thoughts, and "getting up, obeyed the monitor without reply as without delay" (p.91).

Questions on Chapter Six

1. Which details develop the picture of the girls' everyday life at Lowood in this chapter?
2. How are the two teachers contrasted in their methods and personality?

3. How do Jane and Helen differ in their feelings and attitudes to their situation?

Glossary

P.86   Unavailing: useless
P.86   Impotent: powerless
P.88   Smart: pain, discomfort
P.88   Provoking: irritating
P.90   Vengeance: retaliation
P.91   Abyss: chasm, vast deep gorge

Chapter Seven

Summary

The pupils of Lowood spend a miserable Sunday at church, and the routine of that day is described. Mr Brocklehurst and his female relatives visit the school and he warns the pupils and staff against the bad influence of Jane, his impressions being formed by Mrs Reed's account of her.

Commentary

The discomforts of Sundays at Lowood are described, and Mr Brocklehurst's disciplinarian attitude is made clear. The day of the week which would normally be expected to bring relief for the girls from the harshness of the daily rituals proves to be even worse. The church visits they make are tedious and uncomfortable; the suffering from the cold weather is intense. The author vividly describes the terrible soreness of chilblained feet: "the torture of thrusting the swelled, raw and stiff toes into my shoes in the morning" (p.92). The whole day is spent at the church, as it was too far away from school to go back for a meal, and the same inadequacy of food does little to sustain the girls: "an allowance of cold meat and bread, in the same penurious proportion observed in our ordinary meals, was served round between the services" (p.92).

Apart from the deprivations of poor and inadequate food, the younger girls are bullied by the older ones into giving up part of their meal, and through the descriptions of the "great girls" and their treatment, and the harshness of the weather, the author creates a dismal and unhappy picture of the life they are forced to lead, not even having the solace of warmth on their return as "each hearth in the schoolroom was surrounded by a double row of great girls" (p.93).

Mr Brocklehurst's visits reinforce the impression already gained of him as a stern and inhumane disciplinarian; as previously he is described not as a person but an awful presence; his approach is described in terms of a "gaunt outline" and "a long stride" (p.93). Jane's dread of his coming is made clear; every day she had feared that his "information respecting my past life and conversation was to brand me as a bad child for ever" (p.94), relecting Mrs Reed's unjust report to him when he visited Gateshead.

The meanness of Mr Brocklehurst is shown clearly by his concern about even such mundane things as sewing needles: "not, on any account, to give out more than one at a time to each pupil"; pinafores: "the rules limit them to one"; and finally, "no such meal as lunch mentioned" (pp.94 - 95). This concern for the rigid observance of the rules, which he himself no doubt instituted, illustrates the hypocrisy which is emphasised further when he suggests the very deprivations he is forcing the girls to endure are done with a concern for "... the spiritual edification of the pupils, by encouraging them to evince fortitude under the temporary privation" (p.95), whereas he probably gains more money for himself if he keeps a rigid check on expenditure within the school.

This same attitude becomes ludicrous when he turns his attention to the girls' hair, exaggeratedly referring to curls and top-knots as "abundance ... excrescence ... plaits which vanity itself might have woven" (p.96). The contrast between him and Miss Temple with her more humanitarian attitude, is shown as she stares stonily at him after defending her action of ordering replacement breakfast, and during his ridiculous outburst over the girls' hair, has to hide her lips behind her handkerchief "as if to smooth away the involuntary smile that curled them" (p.96).

The visit of Mr Brocklehurst's relatives, and his denunciation of Jane. The hypocrisy of the headmaster is further reinforced by the appearance of his female relative, who are dressed in "velvet, silk and furs" (p.97); clearly he is prepared to spend vast sums on their clothes and keep them in high style while the girls in his charge are half-starved and poorly clad. The power of these people over the staff of the school is awesome, as they are "deferentially received" and "conducted to seats of honour", and listened to respectfully while they detail complaints after their insensitive and intrusive "rummaging scrutiny of the rooms upstairs" (p.97).

Jane's fearful attempt to avoid the attention of the headmaster is foiled by the crash of her slate which she lets fall, and the drama of the resulting command of Mr Brocklehurst, "Let the child who broke her slate come forward!", emphasises the trauma it causes Jane. The frequent exclamation marks, shorter sentences and exaggerated language, "the worst ... paralysed ... dread judge" (p.97), all enforce the powerful effect of the detailed description. The sensitivity of Jane is also further emphasised, when Miss Temple's kind encouragement is felt "like a dagger", as Jane knows she is about to be denounced, and fears the teacher "will despise me for a hypocrite" (p.98).

The vulnerability of the child is shown when she is placed on a high stool, and exposed to the gaze of the whole school, as she sees the "silvery plumage" of Mr Brocklehurst below her and is "hoisted" to the height of his nose. The ability of the author to render skilfully feelings in physical form for the reader to more easily identify is shown once more as the stares of the other pupils, teachers and visitors are described as "directed like burning-glasses against my scorched skin" (p.98).

The exaggerated, dramatic quality of Mr Brocklehurst's language is like that of the 'hell-fire' preachers, as he considers, "Who would think that the Evil One had already found a servant and agent in her?" (p.98). He continues in similarly extreme fashion, warning the girls to avoid such a bad influence, and the teachers "to watch her; keep your eyes on her movements, weigh well her words, scrutinize her actions" (p.98). This repetition of phrasing, balanced and carefully delivered, culminates in the declaration, effectively punctuated to gain the maximum impact, "— this girl is — a liar!" (p.98). The hypocrisy of the adults with whom Jane has had contact is further emphasised by Mr Brocklehurst's description of Mrs Reed, who, as the reader knows, is anything but "the pious and charitable lady" described, and who certiably did not rear Jane "as her own daughter" (p.99).

Again the physical description of Jane's mental suffering is very effective: "stifling my breath and constricting my throat" and similarly of the relief she feels at the gentle smile of Helen, "as if a martyr, a hero, had passed a slave or victim, and imparted strength in the transit" (p.99). The chapter ends with one of the author's many general observations of human attitudes, related to individual characters in the story. Miss Scatcherd cannot see the goodness in Helen because her small faults stand out; eyes like hers are almost pitied as they "can only see these minute defects, and are blind to the full brightness of the orb" (p.99).

Questions on Chapter Seven

1. How do the girls at Lowood spend their Sundays?
2. By what means is Mr Brocklehurst's hypocrisy shown?
3. What positive feelings and experiences help to improve Jane's situation a little?

Glossary

P.92   Penurious: mean, small
P.94   Brand: label, mark
P.95   Edification: improvement

P.95   Evince: show
P.95   Privation: lack, hardship
P.96   Excrescence: outgrowth, projection
P.96   Involuntary: unintentional
P.98   Hypocrite: pretender, false personality
P.99   Pious: religious

Chapter Eight

Summary

Jane is exonerated of the blame attached to her by Mr Brocklehurst; she and Helen have tea with Miss Temple; Helen's illness appears worse; she is punished by Miss Scatcherd for having an untidy drawer.

Commentary

Jane's reaction to Mr Brocklehurst's accusation is described. As previously noted, Jane's reactions tend to be extreme, in direct contrast to Helen Burns' gentle resignation. She feels "ardently I wished to die", is affected by "overwhelming ... grief", wonders "could I ever rise more?" (p.100) and declares she would rather break an arm, be tossed by a bull, or "stand behind a kicking horse, and let it dash its hoof at my chest" (p.101), than lose the affection of those such as Helen and Miss Temple. Helen speaks gently and calmly, and as usual in terms of the world beyond the human, looking always to the spiritual realm, comforting Jane with a vision of heavenly protection, "those spirits watch us, for they are commisioned to guard us" (p.101).

The hints about Helen's illness distract Jane for a while from her own situation, and a foreboding tone is developed by various references to her cough. The scene where Miss Temple comes upon Helen comforting Jane is very dramatic; the moonlight shining on them is a symbol of their innocence and the natural world's reflection of this is extended in Miss Temple's kind attentions. The idea of Miss Temple's room as a haven, a retreat from the harshness of the everyday life of the school is emphasised by the long distance covered to find it, through "intricate passages" (p.102), and the "good fire" represents the warmth and comfort of human love.

Jane tells of her childhood and treatment at Gateshead. Miss Temple's fair and reasonable attitude to Jane and the false story of her evil nature is in contrast to Mr Brocklehurst's tyrannical and avenging accusation, and her invitation to Jane to tell her side of the story is formal and yet encouraging: "You have been charged with falsehood; defend yourself to me as well as you can" (p.102). Jane's continuing development and maturity, charted throughout the novel, is shown again as she learns the lessons imparted by Helen and her example, and she resolves to restrain her emotions: "I infused into the narrative far less of gall and wormwood than ordinary" (p.103).

Again the foreboding relating to Helen is developed in the sigh expressed by Miss Temple after she has taken Helen's pulse, and her deliberately determined cheerfulness as she suggests tea implies that she is troubled and distressed at Helen's condition but does not want to show this. The contrast of Miss Temple with other staff in the institution is shown again in her reaction to the small amount of toast brought up with the tea; the housekeeper refuses more as Mr Brocklehurst would have done. Her offering of cake, and the "generous hand" with which she cuts slices for them, shows her caring nature. The room and the tea tray are described in terms of warmth and light, and the whole episode is like a gleam of brightness in the dull routine of Lowood life.

The treatment of Helen at bedtime is a direct contrast, designed to emphasise further the delight of Miss Temple's kindness and to bring the reader down to earth sharply. Miss Scatcherd's humiliating punishment, "she should have half a dozen of untidily folded articles pinned to her shoulder" (p.105), is received with typically saintly acceptance by Helen, and equally typically resentful anger by Jane, who tore off the label Helen had been forced to wear "and thrust it into the fire" (p.105).

The final confirmation of Jane's true character, obtained by Miss

Temple's communication with Mr Lloyd, is a mirror of the formality of Mr Brocklehurst's denunciation, with all the school assembled and the public declaration that she is "completely cleared from every imputation" (p.106). The end of the chapter suggests both Jane's gradual acceptance of, and adaptation to, Lowood, with far more positive descriptions of the various skills she is able to learn. The possibility of another way of escape from difficulties and deprivation, through painting and drawing, as well as through books, is suggested by the idea of spiritual and intellectual nourishment: "I feasted instead on the spectacle of ideal drawings" (p.106).

Questions on Chapter Eight

1. What events and developments in this chapter make Jane's life more positive and appealing?
2. What contrasting sadness is hinted at, and how?
3. How are Miss Temple and other staff at the school contrasted in this chapter?

Glossary

P.100 Ardently: intensely, fervently
P.101 Commisioned: specially employed, detailed
P.103 Gall, wormwood: bitterness, poison
P.106 Imputation: accusation

Chapter Nine

Summary

Jane develops another friendship; Helen's illness becomes ever graver, and eventually she dies, Jane having spent her last night with her.

Commentary

The sickness and death in the school are contrasted with the better weather and greater freedom enjoyed by Jane and other fitter girls. The frequent references to weather and climate made elsewhere in the novel can be seen here in the description of the welcomed, kindlier season of Spring, and the typical description of the heroine's physical response is shown in the reference to the healing of the chilblains which caused her such suffering during the cold weather, as her feet "began to heal and subside under the gentle breathings of April" (p.107). The school Charlotte Bronte calls 'Lowood' is almost an exact recreation of Cowan Bridge, the school for daughters of impoverished clergy to which she and her sisters were sent, and where they suffered similar deprivations. The illness of Helen Burns is a fictionalised account of the equally desperate state of Charlotte's sister Maria, who died of consumption, or tuberculosis, after having boarded at the school, as did another sister, Elizabeth.

The more positive mood of Jane in response to the brightening weather is shown in the personification of optimism, "... a greenness grew over those brown beds, which, freshening daily, suggested the thought that Hope traversed them at night ..." (p.107). The hills and streams beyond the school walls also take on a more attractive aspect in the better weather. The actual setting for the school building, however, provides a sharp contrast with the appealing description of the surrounding landscape, as it is set in a valley in which fog tends to lie, and the damp atmosphere causes disease to spread amongst the pupils. Again the author uses personification to make the onset and development of illness seem the more vivid and sinister, "That forest dell ... breathed typhus through its crowded schoolroom and dormitory ... disease had thus become an inhabitant of Lowood, and death its frequent visitor ..." (p.108). The irony of the beautiful weather and bright flowers out of doors is emphasised powerfully in the poignant comment: "... these fragrant treasures were all useless ... except to furnish now and then a handful of herbs and blossoms to put on a coffin" (p.108).

The delights of the freedom and better food gained by those girls who remained free of infection as Jane herself did, and the description of the loveliness of the outside world, create another contrast in this chapter. In contrast to those sick and dying in the school, the others "enjoyed fully the beauties of the scene and season" (p.109), and Jane makes another friend, "Mary Ann Wilson, a shrewd, observant personage" with whom Jane has long conversations on the broad stone in the middle of the stream which becomes her special place.

Jane's relationships with her friends, Mary Ann and Helen, are described, and Helen's illness becomes even graver. The author uses direct speech to the reader to emphasise that her heroine does not neglect Helen even though she has found another friend in Mary Ann. A series of questions are asked and answered to enforce the importance of this, culminating in the assurance: "I never tired of Helen Burns, nor ever ceased to cherish her ..." (p.109). The hint of foreboding relating to Helen in previous chapters is reinforced, in the comment about the naivety of Jane in response to her illness, "... her complaint was consumption, not typhus; and by consumption I, in my ignorance, understood something mild ..." (p.110).

This foreboding is increased, again by means of the author's effective use of contrast, in the description of the happy wanderings of Jane and Mary Ann in the wood until nightfall, and the sinister reference to the doctor's horse at the school when they return: "somenone must be very ill, as Mr Bates had been sent for at that time of the evening" (p.110). Jane's fears of Heaven and Hell and her uncertainty, sharpened just at this time, also add to the sense of disturbance, and foreshadow the sense of insecurity which Jane will feel at the loss of Helen. Her mind "felt the one point where it stood — the present; all the rest was formless cloud and vacant depth; and it shuddered at the thought of tottering, and plunging amid that chaos" (p.111).

The short lines of dialogue between Jane and the nurse about the state of Helen break up the narrative and set the truth out starkly, especially the ominous comment: "she'll not be here long" (p.111). Jane's stealthy progress in the middle of the night to visit Helen in Miss Temple's room is described in tense and secretive tone, as she "crept ... dreaded being discovered ... a profound stillness pervaded the vicinity ..." (p.111 - 112). The tension is increased as Jane approaches Helen's bed and fears she may already be dead: "I still recoiled at the dread of seeing a corpse" (p.112). The coldness of Helen's body and her calmness suggest the imminence of death, but Jane is still naive or possibly deliberately attempting to refuse to recognise the truth, as she tries to reassure herself, "she is not going to die" and typically resists Helen's tranquil acceptance of going to "my last home" with cries of "No, no, Helen" (p.112).

Helen's calm tenderness and resignation in death and Jane's last time with her friend are described. Helen's saintly nature is once more made clear in her concern for others rather than herself; even when she is dying she cares for Jane's comfort: "Jane, your little feet are bare: lie down and cover yourself with my quilt" (p.113). Her resignation and acceptance are shown in the calm confidence of her faith, in contrast to Jane's uncertainty and questioning attitude:

"But where are you going to, Helen? Can you see? Do you know?" Helen replies: "I believe; I have faith; I am going to God" (p.113).

The tenderness of the girls' relationship is clearly shown by the gentle words they share and the description of the two lying down together in mutual comfort. The author avoids sentimentality by the earlier rebellious questioning of Jane, not merely accepting Helen's surety. The stark reality of death is slightly muted as the description of Jane being found in the arms of her dead friend is reported through the explanation given later by Miss Temple, rather than in Jane's own words; she was taken away to her own bed without realising immediately what had happened. The final comment of the chapter, about Helen's grave, restores the hopeful and positive mood of the opening, as the single word "Resurgam" (Latin for 'I shall rise again'), later added on a plaque near Helen's "grassy mound", clearly reinforces Helen's ideas of the afterlife and the resurrection to a better world.

Questions on Chapter Nine

1. What uses does the author make of contrast in this chapter?
2. How does the author show the importance of the natural world to the characters in this chapter?
3. How does detailed description add to the creation of different moods in this chapter?

Glossary

P.109 Cherish: care for, hold dear
P.112 Pervaded: filled
P.112 Recoiled: drew back

Chapter Ten

Summary

Jane becomes unsettled at Lowood after the departure, on marriage, of Miss Temple. She advertises for another position and is offered one by a Miss Fairfax of Northfield. After the necessary permission has been obtained from the school and her guardian, Jane is about to leave when Bessie, the maid from Gateshead, comes to visit her. She travels off to a new place and different duties.

Commentary

Jane becomes restless at school after the departure of Miss Temple. The relief and pleasure felt by Jane once the school has been moved to a better building, after the disclosure of the dreadful conditions resulting in the typhus outbreak, can be seen in her comment that "it became in time a truly useful and noble institution" (p.115). Her involvement in the school has made it a secure environment for her in which she feels she can make a real contribution; she has lived there for eight years, "... six as pupil, and two as teacher; and in both capacities I bear my testimony to its value and importance" (p.115).

This security is shattered, however, at the marriage of Miss Temple, though Jane suggests she was happy for her, her husband being "an excellent man, almost worthy of such a wife" (p.116). The school and its surroundings begin to become restricting and confining for Jane, and she sees the distant hills as a symbol of freedom and new life to experience: "I traced the white road winding round the base of one mountain, and vanishing in a gorge between two. How I longed to follow it further! (p.117). The repetition of "liberty" (p.117), suggests the desperation Jane feels, and as she tries to pray for her future she even accepts that another position may bring further imposition on her; nevertheless, she pleads, "grant me at least a new servitude!" (p.117).

Jane advertises for a new position, receives a letter in response from a Miss Fairfax, and just before the journey to the new place of work, encounters Bessie, the maid she knew at Gateshead. As previously, the author effectively expresses Jane's emotional state in physical terms; her frenzied thought and debate within herself cause "pulses (to) throb in my head and temples"; she is "feverish" (p.118), but eventually the idea of placing an advertisement in the local paper is welcomed like "a kind fairy" (p.118), the sense of an external agent encouraging and inspiring her links with the idea of going out and away from the imprisonment she now feels in the school.

The determination of Jane is shown in her disregard for the bad weather as she goes to Lowton to post her advertisement to the paper. Her anticipation and tension in awaiting a reply is suggested in the comment that "The succeeding week seemed long" (p.119); that the woman in the post office seemed to take ages to find any reply: "she opened a drawer and fumbled along its contents for a long time, so long that my hopes began to falter" (p.119); and that she could not read it at once as she had to get back to the school and "various duties awaited me on my arrival" (p.119).

The reader is thus involved in the suspense, and eventually as eager as the character to find out the contents of the letter. Jane's imaginative nature is shown as she tries to conjure up an image of the woman who has written to her and the place where she might work. "Mrs Fairfax! I saw her in a black gown and widow's cap ... Thornfield! ... a neat, orderly spot, I was sure" (p.120).

Once again the tension of suspense is created as Jane has to wait for formal permission to leave the school and permission also has to be granted by Mrs Reed. This emphasises the dependence of Jane on others; she has never had the complete freedom of her own will and desires, but always has to ask others for permission to change her situation. The lack of concern shown by Mrs Reed: "I might do as I pleased" (p.121) could have diminished Jane's self-esteem, but she takes it positively, as she does therefore come a little nearer to governing her own life and interests.

The everyday details of preparations and packing up are described as this is to be a significant change in Jane's life; the sense of another stage on a journey of development of the character is suggested by the use of the trunk as a symbol of Jane's different phases of life; it is "the same I had brought with me eight years ago from Gateshead" (p.121). The connections of one phase with another are embodied in the presence of Bessie, who comes to the school just in time to see Jane before she departs.

The delight with which Jane greets the former maid shows how little family contact she has, and how few friends: "I was embracing and kissing her rapturously" (p.122); she is eager to know all about the people she had left behind, and Bessie's family: "Tell me everything about them, Bessie" (p.122). Bessie's affection for Jane is shown in the fact that she has called her daughter after her, and that she has taken the opportunity to visit her, "I thought I'd just set off, and get a look at you before you were quite out of my reach" (p.123). Her fondness for Jane is also shown in her delight that she equals or exceeds the Reed girls in her accomplishments of piano-playing, painting and speaking French: " 'The Miss Reeds could not play as well!' said she exultingly. 'I always said you could surpass them in learning'" (p.123).

The last part of the chapter introduces an intriguing development, and a hint to the reader of further revelations to come, as Bessie mentions a relative who called for Jane at Gateshead nearly 7 years previously: "he seemed so much disappointed, for he could not stay; he was going on a voyage to a foreign country ..." (p.124). Bessie's staunch defence of Jane's family again shows her liking for her: "... they may be poor; but I believe they are as much gentry as the Reeds are ..." (p.124). The very end of the chapter looks forward, as Jane does, to another stage in her life: "I mounted the vehicle which was to bear me to new duties and a new life" (p.124).

Questions on Chapter Ten

1. How does the author show the difference in Jane's attitude to her life at Lowood before and after Miss Temple's marriage?
2. What realistic details are given about Jane's arrangements to find herself another position?
3. How does the description of the reunion of Bessie and Jane show how they feel about one another?

Glossary

P.115 Capacities: situations, roles
P.117 Servitude: slavery
P.123 Exultingly: delightedly, triumphantly

Chapter Eleven

Summary

Jane's journey to her new place of work is described; she meets Mrs Fairfax and Adele, the little girl she is to teach; she has a tour around Thornfield Hall and hears a strange, chilling laugh coming from one of the upstairs apartments.

Commentary

Jane's journey and her feelings about her new position are described. The author directly addresses the reader through the words of the central character in the opening of this chapter, suggesting the realism of the personality she has created but also reminding the reader that it is a story. The stage set description emphasises this, and also adds to the sense of unreality Jane feels, as if she is taking on another part in her life's play. The immediacy of her situation is suggested by the use of the present tense: "I am not very tranquil ... here I am waiting ..." (p.125).

Having involved the reader more directly in Jane's situation by this device, the author then returns to the past tense and the story continues, with Jane's enquiry and discovery of the carriage and driver awaiting her. She tries to gain an impression of her new employer by considering the carriage which has been sent for her, and is relieved that it is not very extravagant or luxurious, though comfortable, as "I have never lived among fine people but once and I was very miserable with them" (p.126). Jane's dedication and sense of duty is shown in her reflections on her situation, "I will do my best: it is a pity that doing one's best does not always answer" (p.126). This also shows her philosophical attitude to life and her realism; she feels confident in her own worth and recognises that others will not necessarily always value it.

The description of the long drive to Lowton, taking nearer two hours than the original hour and a half suggested by the driver, is made realistic by Jane's attempts to make out details of places that are passed through, and the contrast of the "double illumination of fire and candle" (p.127) with the dark misty night makes the first impression of Thornfield welcoming. The first impressions of Mrs Fairfax are also positive, as she welcomes Jane herself and orders food and drink for her. Jane is pleased but wary: "She treats me like a visitor ... but I must not exult too soon" (p.128).

Jane's first impressions of the house and the manager, Mrs Fairfax, are described. She is confused as to the composition of the household, and has to ask a series of questions to discover any details. There is a combination of negative and positive impressions formed in the introduction of Jane to the new place she is to work in. The confusion of names at first disconcerts Jane: "Varens is the name of your future pupil", but the enthusiasm of Mrs Fairfax, suggesting she will treat Jane as a friend and an equal: " I am so glad you are come; it will be quite pleasant living here now with a companion" (p.128), soon dispels initial uncertainty: "My heart really warmed to the worthy lady ..." (p.129). A glance around the house as she is being shown to her room is at first unnerving: "very chill and vault-like ... cheerless ... space and solitude" (p.129) but again this is dispelled by the attractiveness of the "livelier aspect of my little room" (p.129).

The realism of the character of Jane is emphasised in the description of her consideration of her appearance and her wish to be more attractive, but again her own sensible and direct attitude is shown as she consoles herself: " I thought I should do respectably enough ... and that my new pupil would not at least recoil from me with antipathy" (p.130). The optimistic mood Jane wakes with is reflected in the pleasant weather and attractive scenery: "the early sun shone serenely on embrowned groves and still green fields" (p.130).

The mention of Mr Rochester comes as a surprise to Jane; she has clearly not been given much information as to the household of which she is to become a part: "I had never heard of him before; but the old lady seemed to regard his existence as a universally understood fact" (p.131). She has to gain the facts gradually through a series of questions, that Mrs Fairfax is the manager rather than the owner of Thornfield, that Mr Rochester is the actual owner, and that the little girl she is to teach is Mr Rochester's ward, and speaks more French than English. The first impression of her pupil is a positive one: she is attractive and well mannered, "She came and shook hands with me when she heard that I was her governess ... she suddenly commenced chattering fluently" (p.133).

Jane meets her new pupil and quickly builds up a good relationship with her. The rapport between Adele and Jane is quickly built up through the little girl's delight at being able to communicate in her native tongue. The sense of mystery about the house and its occupants suggested previously by the number of questions Jane had to ask, is added to by the suggestion that Mrs Fairfax does not know about the former life of Adele: "I wish ... you would ask her a question or two about her parents ..." (p.133). The accomplishments revealed by the child, her ability to sing and declaim poetry in a manner very advanced for her years, imply a cultured and intelligent mother, who used to teach Adele but died when the girl was younger even than her 8 years. The disappointment of a child at the activities of adults is shown in her remark about Mr Rochester, who asked if she would like to live with him: "... but you see he has not kept his word, for he has brought me to England, and now he has gone back again himself, and I never see him" (p.134).

Jane's understanding of young children, gained during her time at Lowood, is shown in her sensitivity to Adele's needs: "I felt it would be injudicious to confine her too much at first ... I had talked to her a great deal, and got her to learn a little ..." (p. 135). After her first schoolroom session with Adele, more intriguing aspects of the household are indicated, in the description of the beautiful, light and colourful dining and drawing rooms, "except that the air feels chilly, one would think they were inhabited daily" (p.135). The mystery is further increased when Jane's questions to Mrs Fairfax reveal that she has very little knowledge of her employer: her comments are very vague: "... I suppose ... perhaps ... I should think ... I dare say ... I never had much conversation with him" (p.136).

The mystery of the house and its occupants is increased during the tour given by Mrs Fairfax. The tour of the house which Jane is given by Mrs Fairfax adds yet more of a sense of intrigue and mystery; there are elaborately furnished rooms, past fashions of former years suggested in the items which have been removed to upper stories, and Jane comments: "All these relics gave to the third story of Thornfield Hall the aspect of a home of the past a shrine of memory" (p.137). A sense of unease is introduced when Jane thinks of ghosts, but this is quickly dismissed by Mrs Fairfax's cheery denial. Jane feels at home and content, especially when she looks out over the surrounding scenery from the high attic room: "No feature in the scene was extraordinary, but all was pleasing" (p.138).

Suddenly, towards the end of the chapter, when the author has almost completely reassured the reader, through the discoveries of the heroine, that this is a pleasant and tranquil place to live and work, there comes the disturbing sound of "a curious laugh ... as preternatural a laugh as any I ever heard ..." (p.138). Although Mrs Fairfax hastily attempts to suggest it is only the sound of servants being too boisterous, the impression is given that there is more to be discovered, and although she soon dismisses the feeling, Jane's thought that in other circumstances "I should have been superstitiously afraid", remains to cast a slightly sinister tone over the last part of the chapter.

Questions on Chapter Eleven

1. Give an account of Jane's journey to Lowton and her arrival at Thornfield. How are the details made realistic?
2. What is the first impression gained of Mrs Fairfax?
3. What is Jane's new pupil like, and how does she respond to Jane?
4. What are the grounds and rooms of Thornfield Hall like, and what kind of atmosphere do they have?

Glossary

P.125 Tranquil: calm
P.130 Antipathy: dislike, hostility
P.130 Serenely: calmly
P.135 Injudicious: unwise
P.138 Preternatural: abnormal, supernatural

Chapter Twelve

Summary

Jane settles down into the routine of teaching Adele. She still occasionally hears the sound of 'Grace Poole' and her weird laugh in the upstairs corridors. When she goes for a walk one winter afternoon, as Adele has a cold and cannot have lessons, she meets Mr Rochester without realising who he is; he falls when his horse slips on a patch of ice and Jane offers assistance. When she returns to Thornfield, she recognises the master's dog and realises that he is her absent employer.

Commentary

Jane settles in to a comfortable routine as governess at Thornfield, occasionally disturbed by the sounds of Grace Poole. Once again, she starts to feel restless. Jane has a pleasant life at Thornfield; both Mrs Fairfax and Adele are friendly and reasonable. Despite this, she is sometimes restless, and when she wanders round the house and looks out to the horizon from the upper storeys, she "longed for a power of vision which might overpass that limit; which might reach the busy world ..." (p.140). As in previous chapters, Jane's imaginative nature is shown, through the fantasy worlds she dreams up. She is "quickened with all of incident, life, fire, feeling" that she desired and did not have in her existence (p.141).

Jane's independent spirit is also emphasised in this chapter, and the author's feelings, expressed through her character, about the need for women's education are made clear. She feels fervently that women should not merely be seen fit for "making puddings and knitting stockings ... It is thoughtless to condemn them, or laugh at them, if they seek to do more or learn more than custom has pronounced necessary for their sex" (p.141).

The strange character of Grace Poole, to whom Mrs Fairfax attributed the peculiar laugh Jane heard, is seen occasionally and Jane is led to believe that the odd mutterings she has heard are the result of the woman's drinking too much, as she is often seen "bearing a pot of porter" (p.142).

Jane goes for a walk and meets a stranger, on the way to the village of Hay, who turns out to be Mr Rochester, her absent employer.

The description of the countryside in winter is beautifully detailed, as the walk Jane takes to Hay is described. The motionless scene is almost as if under a spell, "... the stripped hawthorn and hazel bushes were as still as the white worn stones which causewayed the middle of the path ... the little brown birds, which stirred occasionally in the hedge, looked like single russet leaves that had forgotten to drop" (p.142 - 143).

The contrast of this stillness and Jane's musings on the faraway sounds of small streams with the noise of an approaching horseman is shocking, "A rude noise broke out on these fine ripplings and whisperings ..." (p.143). Jane's imagination is in this circumstance a hindrance, as she begins to think of ghostly stories she has heard in the past from Bessie, and becomes very nervous. The dog she eventually sees fits in with these tales, of the ghostly creature the Gytrash, "a lion-like creature with long hair and a huge head" (p.144) but she is reassured when the rider comes into view, "... the human being, broke the spell at once. Nothing ever rode the Gytrash" (p.144).

First impressions of Mr Rochester, though Jane does not know it is him, are of a strong, powerful figure with "considerable breadth of chest ... stern features and a heavy brow ..." (p.145). Jane's lack of emotional experience and physical closeness to men is shown as she is glad he does not seem attractive to her and is only thus able to offer help: "the frown, the roughness of the traveller set me at my ease" (p.145). It is ironic that Jane does not know the identity of the traveller, as he has a conversation with her about himself and his house! The only clue he gives, and that the author gives the reader, is that he tries to see how she would fit into the household, and when she says she is the governess, he suggests he has known of a governess appointed on his behalf, "deuce take me if I had not forgotten!" (p.146). Jane's dutiful attitude is shown as she tries to catch hold of the horse's bridle, "I should have been afraid to touch a horse when alone, but when told to do it, I was disposed to obey" (p.146).

Jane's restlessness overcomes her again and she feels her life is very dull, but as she returns to Thornfield, the house seems brighter and more lively. There is a hint of later encouragement and development of Jane's abilities through Mr Rochester, as she feels delighted to have been "needed and claimed"; her action "was yet an active thing" (p.147). Clearly she has found her existence at Thornfield, though pleasant, rather stifling and lacking in interest and challenge. She refers to her "monotonous life", and when she returns to the house it is to expectations of "stagnation ... lonely little room ... tranquil Mrs Fairfax ... a uniform and too still existence" (p.147).

Jane's restlessness is again emphasised as she approaches the house, "both my eyes and spirit seemed drawn from the gloomy house ... to that sky expanded before me ..." (p.148). In contrast, the house seems much livelier with the return of Mr Rochester; once she actually enters, she is greeted by "a warm glow ... a genial fire ... pleasant radiance ... cheerful mingling of voices ..." (p.148). Jane only realises that the master of the house and the rider she has helped are one and the same when she sees the almost supernatural creature, the dog Pilot, in the incongruous setting of the homely fireside: "he looked an eerie creature to be alone with ..." (p.148).

Questions on Chapter Twelve

1. What kind of lifestyle does Jane have at Thornfield?
2. Show how Charlotte Bronte makes effective use of natural description in this chapter.
3. What are the first impressions given of Mr Rochester, the "traveller"?

Glossary

P.142 Porter: dark sweet ale
P.144 Gytrash: fairytale creature - a huge ghostly dog

Chapter Thirteen

Summary

Jane and Adele take tea with Mr Rochester. Jane tells him of her former life and her feelings about Lowood and Mr Brocklehurst, then shows him her paintings. She obtains some vague information from Mrs Fairfax about the family problems of her employer.

Commentary

The presence of Mr Rochester makes the house much more alive; Adele is difficult to control because of her excitement; Jane and Adele are summoned to have tea with Mr Rochester. The lively atmosphere suggested in the previous chapter continues to alter Thornfield, and at last Jane feels that there is some connection with the outside world, "a rill from the outer world was flowing through it" (p.150). The natural image used to describe the visitors emphasises the relief Jane feels to escape from the claustrophobic mood she was previously in, even though the callers have all come to see Mr Rochester, and have nothing directly to do with her.

Adele, usually a very obedient pupil, is affected by the change too, and cannot sit still to her lessons. The description is very realistic, as she "kept running to the door and looking over the bannisters" (p.150). The disruption to the usually too ordered and quiet life of the house is reflected in the weather, as so often the situations in the characters' world are paralleled in nature: "The afternoon was wild and snowy ... Twilight and snowflakes together thickened the air" (p.150).

The formality of Mr Rochester is shown in the request that Jane and Adele "would take tea with him in the drawing-room" (p.151), and the suggestion from Mrs Fairfax that Jane should change: "This additional ceremony seemed somewhat stately" (p.151). Jane's slight resentment of the imposition is shown in the hint of sarcasm in this comment, and her later reflection that "it was rather a trial to appear thus formally summoned in Mr Rochester's presence" (p.151).

Mr Rochester conducts a formal interview with Jane, asking about her background; she tells him of her past life and years at Lowood. Mr Rochester seems most impressive and imposing to Jane as she meets with him in the drawing room. With "broad and jutty eyebrows ... grim mouth, chin and jaw ..." (p.151), he seems as immoveable and forceful as Mr Brocklehurst had been, described as a black pillar. Mr Rochester is like a huge stone figure, "his shape ... harmonised in squareness with his physiognomy" (p.151). His imposing formality relaxes rather than disturbs Jane, as when she met him on the road her low opinion of herself and her lack of experience in social life are shown as she suggests , "I could not have returned or repaid (politeness) by answering grace and elegance on my part ..." (p.152). The resemblance to a block of stone is confirmed in Jane's further comment: "He went on as a statue would, that is, he neither spoke or moved" (p.152).

Jane's deprived childhood and lack of comforts or pleasures is shown when she responds to Mr Rochester's questions about presents: "I hardly know, sir; I have little experience of them; they are generally thought pleasant things" (p.152). There seems to be a hint of sarcasm in the tone of Jane's words here, as if she is lightly ridiculing the excessively formal approach of her employer; she continues in somewhat exaggerated response, "a present has many faces to it ... one should consider all, before pronouncing an opinion as to its nature" (p.153). Her genuine desire to serve and enhance the education of her pupil is also shown, as she suggests that approval of Adele's achievements is the best present she could have.

There is a slight sense of the supernatural, connected with the reference to the ghostly appearance of Pilot the dog in the previous chapter, when Mr Rochester unbends slightly at the surprise that Jane had survived eight years at Lowood, "No wonder you have rather the look of another world ... When you came on me in Hay Lane last night, I thought unaccountably of fairy tales ..." (p.153). This is extended in the references to her possibly having bewitched his horse, and to "the men in green" (p.154). Later, Mr Rochester comments that the paintings Jane has done are "elfish" (p.158).

The conversation between Jane and Mr Rochester (p.154), as he asks her questions, has an abrupt and challenging air, almost as if each is testing the other; the sentences are short and sharp, both in his enquiries and in her responses. Jane is direct and uncompromising in her assessment of the Lowood director, "I disliked Mr Brocklehurst; and I was not alone in the feeling. He is a harsh man; at once pompous and meddling" (p.155). The abruptness of the conversation continues, as Mr Rochester "demanded" responses; later he realises this and shows a little more sensitivity: "Excuse my tone of command; I am used to say, 'Do this,' and it is done" (p.155), but his comment is still in the form of a command rather than a request.

Mr Rochester asks Jane about her accomplishments and wants to see her paintings. Jane describes the contents of the scenes she has painted, and after she is dismissed, learns from Mrs Fairfax some vague ideas of problems Mr Rochester has which might account for his uncivil behaviour. Jane's spirited nature is shown again, as in her previously direct responses to Mr Rochester's questions, when he has been rather patronising about her abilities. She suggests he would notice if her work was not original, "I will say nothing, and you shall judge for yourself, sir" (p.156). There is nothing actually insolent in her words but the implication is of a feeling of resentment at his attitude. Again the questions and answers in the next conversation are similarly abrupt, and the idea that Jane is deliberately matching the tone of her employer is confirmed in the difference in tone as she confides to the reader, "they are nothing wonderful" (p.156).

The scenes depicted in Jane's paintings recall those in the book she was looking at at the opening of the novel; they are of wild, cold, landscapes, with sea, wind and cloud. The dark and sombre mood of each is suggested throughout the description, "clouds low and livid ... a cormorant, dark and large ... a drowned corpse ... dim peak of a hill ... sky, dark blue ... iceburg piercing a polar winter sky ... the glassiness of despair ..." (p.157). The images seem to be the author's implication of the psychological state of her heroine, for in each of these dark and rather dreadful scenes, there is a suggestion of one gleam of brightness or light, which might be the more challenging life, or the hope of happiness, for which Jane craves. In the first painting the cormorant held "a gold bracelet"; in the second the woman's shape is "crowned with a star"; in the third "gleamed a ring of white flame" (p.157). Jane's ability to escape into a fantasy world, also suggested at the beginning of the novel, is shown when she paints as she says it is "one of the keenest pleasures I have ever known" (p.157). Mr Rochester confirms this as he suggests, "I dare say you did exist in a kind of artist's dreamland ..." (p.158).

Mr Rochester's intense difficulty in showing emotion, as shown in his very formal manner, is enforced again when he wishes Adele good night; he can hardly bear her natural affection, "he endured the caress, but scarcely seemed to relish it" (p.159). This prompts Jane's remark to Mrs Fairfax, "... he is very changeful and abrupt" (p.159), and her vague remarks in response, "... he has painful thoughts, no doubt, to harass him ... Family troubles ..." (p.159). This increases the suspense and the uncertainty in the reader, the feeling that all is not well in this household even though the lifestyle is calm and comfortable. Further prompting by Jane does not lead to any real enlightenment, "... some steps were taken that were not quite fair ... combined to bring Mr Edward into what he considered a painful position ... now for many years he has led an unsettled kind of life ..." (p.159). All these comments are very indefinite; the reader is left only with a sense of trouble and family conflict, identifying with the feelings of Jane herself, as the author intends.

Questions on Chapter Thirteen

1. What further impressions of Mr Rochester's character and attitudes are given in this chapter?
2. How is Jane's spirited nature suggested?
3. Use your own words to describe in detail the scenes Jane had painted.
4. How is an element of the supernatural and the mysterious introduced in this chapter?

Glossary

P.150 Rill: stream
P.151: Physiognomy: facial appearance

Chapter Fourteen

Summary

Jane and Mr Rochester have a conversation during which a
further sense of mystery is established about his previous life and
the difficulties and problems he has had to contend with. Jane shows
some of her resilient spirit and is admired by Mr Rochester for her
independence.

Commentary

*Jane and Adele are summoned to the dining room; while Adele
examines her present, Mr Rochester explains his need for conversation.* When Jane tidies Adele and checks her own appearance
before going to see Mr Rochester as requested, her description of
herself seems somewhat sarcastic, as if beneath the contained
exterior there is a more lively and spirited person than she allows to
appear: "... all being too close and plain, braided locks included, to
admit of rearrangement" (p.160).

Mr Rochester's formal and exaggeratedly restrained behaviour
is shown in his curt demands of Jane and Adele; his insistence that
the child should not "bother me with any details" of her delight over
the doll he has bought her and his dismissive reference to the "prattle
of children" (p.161) also emphasise this. As in previous conversations with Jane, he seems irritated by the need to try to be at all
pleasant: "Confound these civilities! I continually forget them"
(p.161).

The description of the luxury of the room is similar to Jane's
appreciation of the comfort and warmth emanating from the house
when she returned from her excursion to Hay; this emphasises the

lack of comfort she experienced as a child as she always notices such details and is grateful for them. She refers to "lustre ... festal breadth of light ... curtains hung rich and ample ... the lofty window ..." (p.161-162); the language captures the sense of wonder and delight at such surroundings compared to the privations of Lowood and Gateshead Hall.

The repetition of Jane's references to Mr Rochester's eyes shows that she is attracted to him; even though in her conversation with him she says he is not handsome, she clearly finds him fascinating: "his great dark eyes; for he had great dark eyes, and very fine eyes too ..." (p.162). When he asks her if she finds him handsome, the abrupt question takes her aback, but although she explains she was startled and accidentally said 'no', there seems to be an underlying sarcasm in the comment about the conventional reply she ought to have made, as if she rather despises the convention: "I ought to have replied that it was not easy to give an impromptu answer to a question about appearances ... or something of that sort" (p.162).

She is sharp and perceptive in her responses to Mr Rochester's questions, and although she suggests she might be impertinent in her reactions, she still asks,"You would, perhaps, think me rude if I inquired in return whether you are a philanthropist?" (p.163). She thus suggests that his dismissive manner towards Adele and Mrs Fairfax is unkind, and he clearly acknowledges her perception, as he refers to her effect on his conscience as "another stick of the penknife" (p.163). Jane's resentment at her employer's insistent questions about his attractiveness and intelligence is shown in her reaction to his inquiry as to whether she feels he could change his hardened attitudes: "... how could I tell whether he was capable of being retransformed?" (p.163).

Mr Rochester's arrogant and selfish use of Jane to provide him with a companion on a wet dull night is shown in the commanding and insensitive language he uses: " I am disposed to be gregarious and communicative tonight ... you, I am persuaded, can suit me ...

I have almost forgotten you since ... therefore speak" (p.164).
Jane's recognition of this attitude is clear in her reaction: "Instead
of speaking I smiled; and not a very complacent or submissive smile
either". There is a battle of wills going on beneath the civilised
surface of their confrontation, and Mr Rochester seems to acknowledge and admire Jane's resilience, as he realises "I put my request
in an absurd, almost insolent form" (p.164).

*As the conversation progresses, Mr Rochester reveals a difficult
and troubled past as an excuse for his brusqueness and lack of tact
and civility. His appreciation of Jane develops from regard to a hint
of tenderness.* Mr Rochester has clearly been shaken by Jane's
reaction to his demanding approach, and tries to explain his attitude:
"I don't wish to treat you like an inferior" (p.164). His request is
rephrased much more gently, "I desire you to have the goodness to
talk to me a little now ..." (p.164), and his suffering is implied in the
unpleasant image of the pain his thoughts give him if he allows
himself to dwell on the past: "cankering as a rusty nail" (p.164). This
image of disease and decay is very powerful, suggesting a gradual
process of some difficulty or unpleasantness constantly wearing
away his contentment.

Jane's answers to Mr Rochester are very direct and sensible; she
again shows her independence of spirit in not immediately responding in exactly the way he expects: "... how do I know what will
interest you? ... Do as you please, sir ... I don't think, sir, you have
the right to command me ... your claim to superiority depends on the
use you have made of your time and experience" (p.165). She shows
her gratitude that he is beginning to see her as a woman with an
individual personality rather than just an employee, as he has
forgotten that she is paid to do his bidding; she will accept his
overbearing ways to some extent "... on the ground that you did
forget it, and that you care whether or not a dependent is comfortable in his dependency ..." (p.165).

Mr Rochester's admiration for Jane develops during the conversation; he compliments her on her manner which was "frank and sincere" (p.166), yet he then seems to feel he has allowed her too much, and partially retracts his comment, fearing he has betrayed his positive feelings towards her: "for what I yet know, you may be no better than the rest ..." (p.166). Jane's reaction, though unspoken, again shows her quick wit and lack of submissiveness: " 'And so may you,' I thought" (p.166). Jane's sympathetic nature and her responsiveness to others are noted by Mr Rochester; he shows how he is beginning to value her in this capacity himself: "... people will instinctively find out, as I have done, that it is not your forte to tell of yourself, but to listen while others talk of themselves" (p.167).

Throughout the conversation between Jane and her employer, the impression is built up of a mysterious past; he refers variously to difficulties and problems without ever actually telling what is on his mind. Thus the author creates a sense of anticipation and suspense in the reader: "I have battled through a varied experience" (p.165); "I have a past experience ... ill-fortune and adverse circumstances" (p.166); "... fate wronged me ... hampered, burdened, cursed as I am ..." (p.167). Jane's commonsense answers attempt to divert her master from any wrongdoing, as he suggests some means by which he might be relieved of his burden which would not be right; again, all is very vague so the reader is left guessing. Mr Rochester tries to justify his idea: "I scarcely think the notion that flitted across my brain was an error ... it has put on the robes of an angel of light" (p.168). Jane counteracts this by warning him, "Distrust it, sir; it is not a true angel ... I judged by your countenance, sir; which was troubled when you said the suggestion had returned upon you" (p.168). Jane's dutiful approach to life is clear in her advice: "... if from this day you began with resolution to correct your thoughts and actions, you would in a few years have laid up a new and stainless store of recollections ..." (p.168). The reader shares Jane's sense of uncertainty in the later part of the conversation; there are various remarks about rules and power which suggest Mr

Rochester is battling with his conscience over some ethical question, but in the end Jane confesses herself "out of my depth" (p.168), and "bewildered" (p.169).

Mr Rochester clearly appreciates Jane's kindly and down-to-earth responses, referring to her "grave quiet manner" (p.169), yet he also shows sufficient perception to understand that Jane's true nature and full potential have been repressed: "The Lowood constraint still clings to you somewhat; controlling your features, muffling your voice, and restricting your limbs ..." (p.169). This is further emphasised in the image of the creature longing for freedom, "I see at intervals the glance of a curious sort of bird through the close-set bars of a cage ..." (p.170). Mr Rochester's regret for his lost youth and the hint that he might restore it through association with Jane is suggested at the end of the passage, despite his comment being directed on the surface towards Adele, "I have been green too, Miss Eyre - ay, grass green: not a more vernal tint freshens you now than once freshened me. My Spring is gone, however, but it has left me that French floweret on my hands ..." (p.171). There is also a further hint here about Mr Rochester's past, and his former love for Adele's dead mother.

Questions on Chapter Fourteen

1. What further information about Mr Rochester's character is gained from this chapter?
2. How does Jane show her spirited yet sympathetic personality in this chapter?
3. What evidence is there during the conversation that Mr Rochester's past has been difficult and mysterious?

Glossary

P.161 Prattle: chatter
P.161 Lustre: glow
P.162 Ample: plentiful
P.164 Gregarious: outgoing, sociable
P.164 Cankering: infecting, corrupting
P.166 Adverse: difficult, unfavourable
P.167 Instinctively: naturally
P.167 Forte: main strength or ability
P.167 Hampered: overwhelmed, troubled
P.171 Vernal: springlike, fresh

Chapter Fifteen

Summary

Jane learns from Mr Rochester of his relationship with Adele's mother. More developments in understanding the strange character of her employer encourage Jane to enjoy his company. She hears again the strange laugh she has been told is Grace Poole and wakes to find Mr Rochester's bedroom on fire, from which she saves him.

Commentary

Mr Rochester tells the story of his relationship with Adele's mother and how she rejected him for another man. The chapter begins with a reference to Mr Rochester's promise to explain his connection with Adele, and the romantic story of betrayed love he tells, despite his derision ("I began the process of ruining myself in the received style, like any other spoony") (p.172), adds to Jane's and the reader's sympathy for him. His description of the room he had supplied for Celine, the opera singer who was Adele's mother, hints at distressing discoveries to come, as he refers to the oppressive atmosphere: "I was just beginning to stifle" (p.172), and admits that "I never thought there was any consecrating virtue about her" (p.172).

The description of the scene as "very still and serene" prepares for the destruction of that serenity and the fact that Mr Rochester takes a cigar as he tells the story, just as he did at the time, suggests he is and was in need of a calming influence. As his story continues, the reader is prepared for the revelation of Celine's unfaithfulness by the detail of her being "muffled in a cloak — an unnecessary encumbrance" (p.173), and "a figure jumped from the carriage after

69

her: cloaked also ..." (p.173).

When Mr Rochester breaks off his story to contemplate Jane's lack of experience, the imagery used is very wild and frightening, adding to other suggestions in earlier chapters that Mr Rochester's experience of emotional situations has been harsh and difficult. He refers to "rocks bristling ... breakers boil ... a craggy pass ... broken up into whirl and tumult ..." (p.173). Other sinister hints are given as he looks at the house and avoids explaining what it harbours which makes him shudder, "... how long have I abhorred the very thought of it, shunned it like a great plague-house? How do I still abhor — ... Some hated thought seemed to have him in its grip ... Lifting his eyes to its battlements, he cast over them a glare ..." (p.173). The author keeps the reader in suspense, not revealing what or who has connections with that part of the house to cause such a reaction.

The resumption of the story shows the intensity of Mr Rochester's feelings, as he refers graphically to the "green snake of jealousy" which "ate its way in two minutes to my heart's core" (p.174), and later to the dismissal of it when he realises neither the woman nor her alternative lover are worth his consideration: "the fang of the snake jealousy was instantly broken ..." (p.175). As in a previous chapter he compliments Jane on her discretion and receptive manner, "... you, with your gravity, considerateness, and caution, were made to be the recipient of secrets" (p.174). This shows his increasing confidence in her company and his regard for her.

Jane's regard for Mr Rochester increases as his kindness is shown and he becomes more relaxed in her company. When Mr Rochester completes his story about finding Celine and her other lover together and fighting a duel the next day, his generosity is shown, even though he has tried to suggest previously that he has no time for children and their needs. He insists that he has no obligation to Adele, "I see no proofs of such grim paternity ... I acknowledged no natural claim on Adele's part ... I am not her father ..." (p.176) and yet he admits, "hearing that she was quite destitute, I e'en took the poor thing out of the slime and mud of Paris, and transplanted it here ..." (p.176). Jane's fierce protectiveness of Adele when Mr Rochester suggests she may no longer wish to care for her now that she knows of her background, shows her connecting Adele's lack of family with her own. She would be likely to be more sympathetic to a child in similar circumstances as she can understand the sense of loss which might be felt, "Adele is not answerable for either her mother's faults or yours ... I shall cling closer to her than before" (p.176).

The continuing development of positive feeling for Jane and her equally positive response shows Mr Rochester's kinder nature, to link with his care of Adele. Jane notices "he always had a word and sometimes a smile for me ... I was honoured by a cordiality of reception ... these evening conferences were sought as much for his pleasure as for my benefit" (p.177). He also broadens her horizons, satisfying for the time her desire for exploration beyond the narrow confines of her experience, "I had a keen delight in receiving the new ideas he offered ... following him in thought through the new regions he disclosed ..." (p.177). The suggestion that their relationship is eventually to be far closer is made in the reference to her reaction that "I felt at times as if he were my relation rather than my master ...", and "I ceased to pine after kindred ..." (p.177). Jane's growing affection for her employer does not blind her to his faults, but she comes to be more understanding of his moods and more than ever convinced, with the reader, of some dark secret which oppresses him, "some cruel cross of fate" (p.178).

Jane hears the wierd laugh again, discovers Mr Rochester's bedroom on fire, and attributes the cause to Grace Poole. The laugh which wakes Jane is chilling in its eerieness. It is described in physical terms, as frequently used in earlier chapters, as "marrow-freezing" (p.179). The eerie and sinister nature of the sound is enforced by the descriptive language of the supernatural:

"a demoniac laugh ... the goblin-laughter ... the unnatural sound ..." (p.179), and by the consideration Jane makes in attributing the laugh to Grace Poole, "is she possessed with a devil?" (p.179). The discovery of the fire is described in realistic stages, as Jane first notices candles burning "... just outside, and on the matting in the gallery"; then "... a strong smell of burning"; then "... the smoke rushed in a cloud ..." (p.179).

The speed and frantic effort of Jane to quench the flames and wake Mr Rochester are conveyed very vividly: "... in an instant, I was within the chamber ... Not a moment could be lost ... I rushed to his basin and ewer ... flew back to my own room ..." (p.179 - 80). It is interesting that Charlotte Bronte turns the traditional heroic rescue around by making the woman the dominant character, as "Mr Rochester lay stretched motionless, in deep sleep" (p.179). Jane's strength of character has always been stressed and through her, the author shows the need for a woman to fulfil her potential and develop her personality as much as a man. Mr Rochester's dazed and muddled reaction to the "shower-bath" of the water Jane threw over him to quench the fire shows he has been made suspicious and cynical by earlier experiences, as he assumes the worst, "Have you plotted to drown me?" (p.180). His references to "elves ... witch, sorceress" (p.180), recall those terms used by Jane of the sound of what she assumes is Grace Poole's laugh, and later she continues to attribute the cause of the fire to the servant's vindictiveness and is puzzled by the fact that Mr Rochester takes no steps to dismiss her.

The mystery of the fire and the strange laughter Jane has heard is increased by Mr Rochester's insistence that no one else should be informed of the incident. Jane notices his expression is of "more concern than astonishment" (p.180) at the events she relates, and he instructs her to "just be still ... be as still as a mouse ... say nothing about it" (p.180-181). His tone is "rather ... peculiar" when he asks if she saw anything apart from the candlestick as she discovered the fire and he seizes on Jane's assumption that the laugh came from

Grace Poole and quickly confirms it: "Just so. Grace Poole — you have guessed it" (p.181).

Mr Rochester's increasing interest in, and respect for, Jane is shown in a variety of ways: as he tries to stop her leaving even though he has dismissed her; in his concern for more direct contact; "... you walk past me as if we were mutual stangers! At least shake hands"; in his pleasure in being obliged to her for his safety, "I feel your benefit no burden, Jane"; in his conviction that she is destined to be a positive influence in his life, his "good genii"; finally in his tender farewell, "My cherished preserver, good-night!" (p.182). The "strange energy ... in his voice, strange fire in his look" (p.182), which Jane notices is probably as much in response to his desirous feelings for her as to the agitation caused by the threat to his security which the fire posed.

Jane is shown to be apparently innocent of the emotional under-current in Mr Rochester's relationship with her, but the author shows her subconscious response to it which she tries to suppress, through description of her uneasy thoughts: "Till morning dawned I was tossed on a buoyant but unquiet sea, where billows of trouble rolled under surges of joy ... Sense would resist delirium: judgement would warn passion" (p.182).

Questions on Chapter Fifteen

1. Retell in your own words the story of Mr Rochester's betrayal by Adele's mother.
2. How is the increasing mutual respect and concern of Mr Rochester and Jane shown in this chapter?
3. How does the author add to the mystery of Thornfield and the strange atmosphere in this chapter?

Glossary

P.172 Spoony: foolish or silly person

P.173 Encumbrance: burden, hindrance

P.173 Abhorred: hated, detested

P.176 Paternity: fatherhood

P.176 Destitute: in utter poverty, with no means of support

P.177 Cordiality: pleasant friendliness

P.177 Pine: long for, yearn

P.180 Ewer: jug

P.182 Mutual: shared, reciprocal

P.182 Buoyant: lively

P.182 Delirium: hallucinatory madness

Chapter Sixteen

Summary

Jane is confused and disturbed by the lack of any sense of guilt in Grace Poole and of any attempt to dismiss or even reprimand the woman she believes to have caused the fire. She is also disturbed by her complicated feelings towards Mr Rochester and longs all day to see him again. She eventually learns that he has gone to visit friends, one of whom is described as a beautiful young woman whom Jane imagines as an appropriate match for Mr Rochester in contrast to herself.

Commentary

Jane is puzzled by the lack of any action taken against Grace Poole and the woman's calm behaviour, and tries to test her on her reaction to the night's events. Jane's uncertainty about the developing relationship between herself and her employer is emphasised by her confused feelings: "I wanted to hear his voice again, yet feared to meet his eye" (p.183). She has clearly kept her word to him about her part in the rescue as the servants' conversation shows they believe Mr Rochester to have both started and put out the fire.

Grace Poole's calm behaviour bewilders Jane; she is contributing to the refurbishment of Mr Rochester's room, "sewing rings to new curtains", and showed in her face "nothing either of the paleness or desperation one would have expected to see marking the countenance of a woman who had attempted murder" (p.183); Jane attempts to stare her out, to force some guilty reaction, but "no increase or failure of colour betrayed emotion, consciousness of guilt, or fear of detection" (p.183).

Charlotte Bronte skilfully suggests the tension and mutual suspicion of Jane and Grace Poole as each tries to draw out the other about their involvement in the events of the previous night. Jane looks at Grace "fixedly"; in return she "seemed to examine me warily"; Jane resolves to "put her to some test" but correspondingly, Grace asks questions of Jane "in a marked and significant tone"; the more Jane tries to find out about Grace's presumed involvement, the more "she appeared to be cross-questioning me ..." (p.184). Jane's persistence in believing that Grace is the cause of "danger or annoyance" (p.185) causes her to misinterpret Grace's concern as malice when she asks if Jane locks her door at night: " 'Fiend! she wants to know my habits, that she may lay her plans accordingly!'" (p.185).

The frustration and irritation caused by Jane's lack of awareness of Grace's real situation are well shown in her summary of her reaction to the woman's behaviour: "I still stood absolutely dumbfounded at what appeared to me her miraculous self-possession and most inscrutable hypocrisy" (p.185). Jane's imaginative nature involves her in mistaken speculations about the relationship between Mr Rochester and Grace Poole: "... what mysterious cause withheld him from accusing her? ... What if a former caprice ... has delivered him into her power ..." (p.186).

Jane considers her feelings for Mr Rochester and longs to speak with him again. Having expected him all day, she eventually learns he has gone to Millcote to see friends, including the beautiful Blanche Ingram. Having thought that Grace Poole might have some hold over Mr Rochester and then dismissing it as unlikely that he would have any emotional dependence on such a plain woman, Jane's fondness for her employer and the jealousy this arouses are shown in her confused feelings. The author refers, through Jane's thoughts, to "the secret voice which talks to us in our own hearts" (p.186), the subconscious emotions which battle with her conscious attempts to deny the feelings and restrain her desires. She considers her own situation in comparison to that she imagines of Grace Poole, and her improved self-image and developing confidence are evident as she thinks, " '*you* are not beautiful either, and perhaps Mr Rochester approves you ... I looked much better than I did when Bessie saw me; I had more colour and more flesh, more life, more vivacity, because I had brighter hopes and keener enjoyments" (p.186-187).

As in previous examples, the author is particularly effective in her description of the ordinary routine of days and the intensity of feeling when some anticipated event is occupying a character's thoughts. Jane's desperation to see Mr Rochester again is clearly shown in the repetition used: "... surely I shall see him before night ... Surely I would not be wholly disappointed tonight" (p.187) and the projection of Jane imagining herself with him, "I fancied sometimes I heard Mr Rochester's own tread ... I knew the pleasure of vexing and soothing him ... that brought me, I imagined, nearer to Mr Rochester's presence" (p.187). This anticipation makes the disappointment of Mr Rochester's absence even more difficult to accept, as shown by the startled reaction: " Journey! — Is Mr Rochester gone anywhere?" (p.188).

Jane's disappointment is intensified when she learns that the company Mr Rochester is keeping includes some attractive young ladies; the description of Blanche Ingram in particular causes unaccustomed jealousy in Jane, which is shown in her insistent questions and deliberate assumption of her attractiveness to Mr Rochester: " Are there ladies at the Leas? ... what was she like? ... She was greatly admired, of course? ... what sort of a voice had she? ... this beautiful and accomplished lady, she is not yet married? ... More unequal matches are made every day" (p.188-189). Jane is shown to be purposefully suggesting Blanche's attractiveness and appropriateness as a match for Mr Rochester to prepare herself and lessen the possible disappointment should this actually be so.

Once again the confusion of Jane's feelings and the battle

between her conscious denial of feelings and subconscious desires are made clear, as she "endeavoured to bring back with a strict hand such as had been straying through imagination's boundless and trackless waste, into the safe fold of common sense" (p.190). The imagery of barren wild landscape reflects the emotional dangers Jane fears in terms of the physical environment, a technique employed by the author with powerful effect. The realism with which she depicts her character's aggressive self-reproach is quite amusing, *"You* of importance to him in any way? Go! your folly sickens me" (p.190).

The reader can easily identify with the struggle Jane has as again physical description illustrates emotional tension, in the image of the fire eating up the soul in unrequited love: "unreturned and unknown, must devour the life that feeds it"; the "miry wilds" of the dangerous landscape of emotions (p.190). Finally the actual action Jane takes of drawing an unflattering picture of herself and a correspondingly appealing picture of the imagined Blanche, physically acts out the situation as Jane forces herself to see it and thus gives her some relief, "I derived benefit from the task: it had kept my head and hands employed ... I was able to meet subsequent occurrences with a decent calm" (p.191).

Questions on Chapter Sixteen

1. What is Jane's attitude towards Grace Poole and how is this shown?
2. How does Jane feel about Mr Rochester, and how does she try to control her feelings?

Glossary

P.183 Countenance: expression
P.185 Dumbfounded: stunned
P.185 Inscrutable: mysterious, incomprehensible
P.187 Vivacity: liveliness
P.190 Miry: marshy, boggy (unclear)

Chapter Seventeen

Summary

The arrangements for company to be received at Thornfield involve great activity. The house party is lavish and glamorous; Jane has to take Adele to be presented to the ladies, who include Blanche Ingram, of whom Jane feels jealous. Mr Rochester hardly seems to notice her.

Commentary

Preparations are made for the entertainment of Mr Rochester's guests. The beginning of this chapter links with the last in describing Jane's difficulty in adjusting to the absence of Mr Rochester. The very insistence of the character in emphasising that "I cleared up the mistake of supposing Mr Rochester's movements a matter in which I had any cause to take vital interest" (p.192), suggests that in fact, she had not been able to do this, and when a letter arrives from the master, her reaction is almost as if it were a personal letter to her: "... a fiery glow ... suddenly rose to my face. Why my hand shook, and why I involuntarily spilt half the contents of my cup into my saucer, I did not choose to consider" (p.193). The retrospective frankness of the narrator makes it clear that she deliberately did not examine her reaction as she knew it was a disturbing and emotional response which she would find difficult to control.

The lively activity of the preparations for Mr Rochester and his guests shows the unfamiliarity of the prospect of a large party and the life and vigour this would give to the house: "... such brushing, such washing of paint and beating of carpets, such taking down and putting up of pictures, such polishing of mirrors and lustres ..."

(p.193); the frequent present participles emphasise the continuity of the action and the importance of the occasion, further underlined as even Jane is involved directly, rather than in keeping Adele out of the way: "From school duties she was exonerated: Mrs Fairfax had pressed me into her service" (p.193).

The continuance of Grace Poole in the house is described as a brooding presence that still disturbs Jane despite her involvement in the liveliness of preparation. Her uncertainty about the woman's role in the household is referred to in dismal, ugly terms, "the region of doubts and portents and dark conjectures", suggesting a sense of foreboding, and her imaginative ideas culminate in an ironic remark, that she is "as companionless as a prisoner in his dungeon" (p.194). Jane's ignorance of Grace Poole's true position is made more apparent by bits and pieces of information that she overhears from the other servants: "she understands what she has to do — nobody better" (p.194) and at this point in the novel the reader is as intrigued by the author's deliberate creation of suspense, as Jane herself is frustrated: "that there was a mystery at Thornfield; and that from participation in that mystery I was purposely excluded" (p.195).

In contrast with the darkness of the imagery connected with the mystery, the decorated cleanliness of the house is presented as shining with light, built up by carefully chosen description, "... radiant ... bright ... polished ... brightness ... resplendent ... bloomed ..." (p.195). Jane enjoys all the activity but the author shows she still has need for personal solitude, into which to withdraw as she had done as a child at Gateshead, into the windowseat, and at Thornfield, into the schoolroom, "a sanctum it was now become to me ..." (p.195).

The guests and their activities are very glamorous, making Jane feel very inferior, especially when Mr Rochester seems to ignore her. The anticipation is skilfully suggested as usual, through Mrs Fairfax's instructions and the eventual announcement:" 'I have sent

John down to the gates to see if there is anything on the road' ...
'They'll be here in ten minutes.' ...The ten minutes John had given
seemed very long ..." (p.195). The description of the first sight of
Miss Ingram is almost regal, the richness of her "purple riding
habit" and the sense of extravagance as this "almost swept the
ground, her veil streamed long on the breeze", together with the
image of beautiful hair, "gleaming ... shone", culminates in the
alliterative spendour of "rich raven ringlets" (p.196). It is as if the
author has deliberately exaggerated the impression given, to reflect
Jane's sense of inferiority in contrast.

A similar exaggeration is used in the description of the preparations in the kitchen as in a fiery furnace, when Jane ventures down
to get herself and Adele something to eat, "all in that region was fire
and commotion ... the cook hung over her crucibles ... threatening
spontaneous combustion" (p.196). The lady guests are seen as
beings from another world; they move "gaily and airily ... gleamed
lustrous ... sweet subdued vivacity ... as a bright mist" (p.197), all
creating an ethereal quality.

Another reminder of the earlier stage of the story at Gateshead is
given when Jane and Adele watch from the gallery and hear the
music coming from below, as Jane used to look on at the comings
and goings of parties from which she was excluded. She is now
excluded from the presence of Mr Rochester, on whom her mind is
still engaged as "my ears were wholly intent on analysing the
mingled sounds and trying to discriminate amidst the confusion of
accents those of Mr Rochester ..." (p.198). Clearly he does not wish
her to be completely excluded, for despite Jane's continual reference to his attentions to Miss Ingram, Mrs Fairfax refers to his
insistence that Jane should come down with Adele, "I shall come
and fetch her in case of contumacy" (p.199). This also shows Mr
Rochester's understanding awareness of Jane's reticence, and his
expectation that she would want to deny herself the chance of
interesting company.

There is a deliberate contrast made between the elaborate preparations made for Adele's presentation to the ladies, "... her curls arranged ... her pink satin frock on, her long sash tied, and her lace mittens adjusted" (p.199) and Jane's quick and simple change emphasised by repetition, "soon put on ... soon smoothed ... soon assumed". When the ladies come through to the room where Adele and Jane are awaiting them, again they are described as beings of a different plane, in this case as exotic creatures, "a flock of white plumy birds" (p.200), or in terms of the mysterious beauty of nature: "all had a sweeping amplitude of array that seemed to magnify their persons as mist magnifies the moon" (p.200).

The narrator runs through a list of names of other ladies to emphasise the importance of the last few, the "three most distinguished ... the Dowager Lady Ingram and her daughters, Blanche and Mary" (p.201). The Dowager provides yet another reminder of Jane's Gateshead days, this time directly acknowledged: "a fierce and hard eye: it reminded me of Mrs Reed's ..." (p.201). Jane's natural honesty and directness which caused her so much trouble at the Reeds' is also reflected in her appraisal of the woman: she notices her "almost insupportable haughtiness in her bearing and countenance" and comments cuttingly on her pretentious clothing: "a shawl turban of some gold-wrought Indian fabric, invested her (I suppose she thought) with a truly imperial dignity" (p.201).

Jane's remarks may well be coloured by the author's suggestions of her jealousy: she is quick to notice the cruelty of Miss Ingram's superiority in conversation over Mrs Dent, who does not know botanical vocabulary, and she seems determined to torture herself by amassing proof of the compatibility of Blanche and Mr Rochester, "... that he *did* admire her, I already seemed to have obtained proof: to remove the last shade of doubt, it remained but to see them together" (p.202). The treatment of Adele by the ladies is also described in terms which suggest Jane's disapproval: "getting spoilt to her heart's content" (p.203), possibly because she herself never had such attention as a child, but more likely to emphasise the patronising attitude of the ladies towards the child, "what a little puppet!" (p.202), very different from Jane's sensible and encouraging approach.

Jane's tension when Mr Rochester enters the room is conveyed vividly by her desperate attempt to concentrate on the bead work she is occupied with, yet being totally unable to think of anything else but how he looks and how different their relationship seems to be in this company from the last time they were alone together. "What had occurred since, calculated to change his and my relative positions? Yet now, how distant, how far estranged we were!" (p.203).

Jane's affection and respect for Mr Rochester are shown in the unfavourable comparisons she makes between him and the gentlemen guests, who might have been considered more conventionally handsome. She sees the others as shallow in contrast, "the light of the candles had as much soul in it as their smile ... his eye grew both brilliant and gentle, its ray both searching and sweet" (p.204). She admits what she has so frequently tried to deny, that she feels some essential bond between herself and Mr Rochester that is far more than mere social affinity, "I feel akin to him — I understand the language of his countenance and movements: though rank and wealth sever us widely, I have something in my brain and heart, in my blood and nerves, that assimilates me mentally to him" (p.204). At last she allows her conscious self to acknowledge "while I breathe and think, I must love him" (p.204).

Jane feels ignored, then ridiculed and despised as she listens to the guests' insensitive comments about governesses. The description of the after-dinner activities of the guests, taking coffee and chatting, is all in the present tense: "conversation waxes brisk and merry ... Frederick Lynne has taken a seat beside Mary Ingram and is showing her the engravings ..." (p.205). This adds to the sense of Jane's exclusion, looking on as at a rich picture, in the room but more or less invisible as far as its other occupants are concerned. Even when Jane is directly referred to as Adele's governess, the indifference of the company to her as an individual is clear in the haughty reference as if to a lower species: "I saw a person ... there she is still ... You pay her ... you have them both to keep ... you should hear Mamma on the chapter of governesses ..." (p.205).

The memories of past governesses in the Ingram household clearly illustrate the ill-mannered and spoilt attitudes of the Ingram children just as much as the weaknesses of the governesses which are recalled. The sweeping generalisation of the Dowager Lady Ingram further emphasises the idea of governesses as being on a lower plane: " 'I noticed her; I am a judge of physiognomy, and in hers I see all the faults of her class' " (p.206); Blanche refers to "... the whole tribe; they are a nuisance" (p.206). Jane's sensitivity to this attitude is shown in the exaggerated language commenting on another guest's reminder "that one of the anathematized race was present" (p.206). Even further evidence of this arrogant and insensitive treatment is shown in the implication that normal human relations should be denied such members of a household, "... there are a thousand reasons why liaisons between governesses and tutors should never be tolerated a moment in any well-regulated house" (p.207).

The worst aspect of this demeaning conversation for Jane is that Mr Rochester, without actually contributing to the comments, does not defend Jane and even seems to agree with Blanche when she suggests a change of topic: "Madam, I support you on this point, as on every other" (p.207). Jane's jealousy of Blanche is shown again as she emphasises the deliberate showiness of Miss Ingram's behaviour: "... both her words and her air seemed intended to excite not only the admiration, but the amazement of her auditors" (p.208). Her distress is shown as she feels she has to leave the room, but her delight in Mr Rochester's singing voice prevents her at first; she is disturbed by its effect on her: "... a mellow, powerful bass, into which he threw his own feeling, his own force; finding a way through the ear to the heart, and there waking sensation strangely" (p.209).

It is only when Jane leaves the room that Mr Rochester comes to her; his concern for her is re-established as he enquires after her health but his insensitivity is also evident as he does not seem to realise how he has hurt her in his indifference: "... a good deal paler than you were - as I saw at first sight. What is the matter?" (p.209). He is still bound by the expectations of his society and class, not wanting to be seen associating himself closely with an employee, "... in mortal dread of some prating prig of a servant passing" (p.210) and stifles an endearment which would have made all the difference to Jane's confidence: " 'Good-night my —' He stopped, bit his lip, and abruptly left me" (p.210). This curt ending to the chapter establishes a desolate tone as the reader feels for Jane in her sense of rejection, in contrast to Mr Rochester's earlier personal confidences in her.

Questions on Chapter Seventeen

1. Describe, in your own words, the preparations made for Mr Rochester's guests at Thornfield.
2. What impression do you gain of Miss Ingram from this chapter?
3. How are Jane's feelings towards the ladies and gentlemen made clear?
4. How does Jane feel about Mr Rochester in this chapter?

Glossary

P.193 Exonerated: released
P.195 Participation: involvement

P.196 Crucibles: containers (that can withstand very hot temperatures)

P.196 Spontaneous: immediate, without any direct cause

P.198 Discriminate: distinguish, sort out

P.199 Contumacy: obstinate resistance, refusal

P.200 Amplitude: extravagance, excess

P.201 Insupportable: unbearable

P.203 Estranged: parted, separated

P.204 Assimilates: incorporates, joins

P.206 Anathematized: detested

P.206 Physiognomy: facial features, expression indicating personality

P.207 Liaisons: relationships

P.208 Auditors: listeners

P.210 Prating prig: gossiping self-righteous person

Chapter Eighteen

Summary

The houseparty guests play charades; one rainy day when Mr Rochester has to go out on business, two visitors arrive at the house: a Mr Mason from Jamaica and a gipsy woman who insists on telling fortunes.

Commentary

Jane describes the charades the guests play and the attentions of Blanche to Mr Rochester. Jane describes the changed atmosphere of Thornfield as the houseparty continues; the guests seem very much part of the household and "there was life everywhere, movement all day long" (p.211). Jane's lack of frivolous entertainment in her life is shown when she says she did not know what charades were, and wonders at the activity of hunting for dressing-up clothes in various old wardrobes in the house. Her feeling of inferiority continues, as even when invited to play by Mr Rochester, she declines and has her reaction reinforced by Lady Ingram's dismissive comment that "she looks too stupid for any game of the sort" (p.212).

The detailed commentary on the scenes presented in the charades adds to the suggestion of Jane having never enjoyed such activities, as she notices every detail. Her description of Mr Rochester's costume in comparison to Miss Ingram's confirms her admiration of the one and jealousy of the other, as she says he "suited the costume exactly: he looked the very model of an Eastern emir ..." (p.212), whereas she only "suggested the idea of some Israelitish princess ... such was doubtless the character she intended to represent" (p.213). The behaviour of Miss Ingram and Mr Rochester is described as very teasing and relaxed, likely to increase Jane's jealousy, especially when he suggests Miss Ingram is his wife as they have acted being married for one of the charade scenes.

Jane, however, insists that she does not feel jealous and frequently repeats that she "could not unlove him" (p.214) despite his attentions to Miss Ingram; she suggests that she could see beneath the surface of Blanche's attractiveness and the shallow woman she recognised was not worth jealousy: "Miss Ingram was a mark beneath jealousy: she was too inferior to excite the feeling" (p.215). It seems as though the author is suggesting that Jane is trying to persuade herself of the truth of her reactions, to convince herself she is not jealous; she still feels she understands Mr Rochester's true nature and that any marriage to Miss Ingram would be only one of convenience: "for family, perhaps political reasons; because her rank and connections suited him; I felt he had not given her his love" (p.215).

Jane's intense feeling for Mr Rochester is made clear as she contemplates how she would feel if Blanche were worthy of her suitor: "I should have had one vital struggle with two tigers — jealousy and despair: then, my heart torn out and devoured, I should have admired her ..." (p.215). The violence of the imagery and the idea of fighting off wild beasts shows how desperate she would feel, but she consoles herself by the thought that Miss Ingram is after all, not worth admiration. Charlotte Bronte is extremely skilful in realistically representing the turmoil of feelings Jane suffers as she sees the man she loves paying court to another woman, yet not really being deeply affected, describing her attempts to charm him as "arrows that continually glanced off from Mr Rochester's breast and fell harmless at his feet" (p.216).

The contrast between Jane's straightforward attitudes and the superficiality of the guests is shown. Jane's genuine feeling and honest emotions are shown, in contrast to the superficiality and pretense of upper class conventions, when she reflects that she has found a gentler side to Mr Rochester which "was not elicited by meretricious arts and calculated manoeuvres;" (p.216). She considers the marriage which she has assumed to be intended between Mr Rochester and Miss Ingram, thinking that surely a gentleman would wish to marry for love, but instead seemed to have to consider "interest and connexions ... All their class held these principles" (p.216). Jane's honest retrospective comments on her feelings at this time show that she realises she was biased: "I was growing very lenient to my master: I was forgetting all his faults ... I saw no bad" (p.217). The continuous artificiality of the party is made clear by the comments on the ladies' reactions in their conversations: "like a pair of magnified puppets", and the actions described as if on stage when the guests "suspended their byplay to observe and listen to the principal actors" (p.217).

The arrival of Mr Mason is typically connected with appropriate weather: it is dull and dismal when he arrives and the idea of underlying uncertainty in connection with him is introduced as he is first mistaken for Mr Rochester, who has gone out to Millcote on business. This mistake on Adele's part, taken up by others, gives an excuse for Blanche to accuse Adele: "you tiresome monkey!" (p.218), as she has previously shown unkindness to the child, probably implying jealousy of Mr Rochester's provision for her. The uncertainty connected with Mr Mason continues with the description of him: "not precisely foreign, but still not altogether English ... something in his face that displeased; or rather, that failed to please" (p.219).

The reader is kept in suspense about the stranger for some time, and as at other points in the novel, made to experience the situation of the main character, as Jane is distracted by a conversation near her between the ladies and only eventually hears fragments of conversation which tell her Mr Mason has come from Jamaica where he met Mr Rochester. This adds to the fascination Mr

Rochester has for Jane: "till now I had never heard a hint given of visits to more distant shores" (p.220).

After the arrival of Mr Mason, the gipsy's visit causes more excitement and her demand to tell fortunes is accepted. The interruption of the gipsy has more sinister undertones than mere entertainment to cheer a dull day; the determination of the woman is very clear; she is referred to as "quite troublesome" (p.220); "insists upon being brought in" (p.220); "says nothing shall stir her" (p.221); she "swears she must and will" tell fortunes (p.221). The attitude of the guests to her appearance is divided between the youngsters who think of it all as a game, "such a chance of fun" (p.221); "it will be excellent sport!" (p.221) and their elders who consider it unseemly: "what are you thinking about? ... such inconsistent proceeding" (p.221); but, as so often, it is Blanche who gets her way: "I must have my will" (p.221).

The references to the strangeness of the gipsy woman by the footman increase the fascination of her for both the characters and the reader: "a shockingly ugly old creature ... she looks such a rough one ... she looks such a tinkler" (p.221-222). Her insistence that she will see only young, single women increases this intrigue, as does the silence of Blanche when she has seen the woman: "she looked neither flurried nor merry; she walked stiffly to her seat, and took it in silence" (p.222). Jane's perceptiveness sees behind this show of unconcern, however: "she herself, notwithstanding her professed indifference, attached undue importance to whatever revelations had been made her" (p.223). The excitement and agitation of the other young ladies add to the tension in the atmosphere, especially when they affirm the truth of her remarks, and all this description culminates in the demand to see Jane, skilfully prepared for by the earlier reference to young single ladies: "she swears she will not go till she has seen all" (p.224). At the end of the chapter, the reader is left in suspense as Jane eagerly agrees to see the gipsy: "I was a good deal interested and excited" (p.224).

Questions on Chapter Eighteen

1. Describe in your own words the game of charades played by Mr Rochester and his guests.
2. How does Jane try to rationalise her feelings about Blanche?
3. What is the first impression given of Mr Mason in this chapter?
4. How does the visit of the gipsy alter the atmosphere of the chapter?

Glossary

P.215 Rank: status
P.216 Elicited: gained, drawn out
P.216 Meretricious: insincere
P.221 Inconsistent: contradictory, irregular
P.222 Tinkler: strange, rough, uncouth person
P.223 Professed: openly expressed

Chapter Nineteen

Summary

Jane goes to the gipsy to hear her fortune and is nearly won over by the uncanny understanding shown of her nature and feelings. Eventually the 'gipsy' is revealed as Mr Rochester in disguise. When Jane tells him of a Mr Mason who has visited the house and stayed to see him, Mr Rochester becomes very agitated and seeks to confirm Jane's support of him.

Commentary

Jane challenges the gipsy over her comments and is eventually persuaded by her apparent knowledge of her thoughts and feelings. The exchange between Jane and the gipsy shows her calm nature and the respect this encourages. Jane is not frightened or particularly excited by what the gipsy might have to say; the short sentences emphasise the directness of the dialogue. Jane seems determined to be sceptical; even when the gipsy seems to describe her situation accurately, she insists: "It would be easy to find you thousands" (p.226) in the same circumstances. However, the gipsy perceptively refers to the contrast Jane had been so aware of between herself and the guests, "just as little sympathetic communion passing between you and them as if they were really mere shadows of human forms and not the actual substance" (p.227).

The gipsy's questions and her connection with Grace Poole disturb Jane: " 'there is diablerie in the business after all, then!'" (p.227). She still connects the servant with the unnatural behaviour at nights in Thornfield, and feels the gipsy's awareness is uncanny. She tries to deny her feelings about Mr Rochester, "they are all at liberty to be the recipients of whose smiles they please, without my feeling disposed to consider the transaction of any moment to me" (p.228). The understanding of the gipsy amazes her: "what unseen spirit had been sitting for weeks by my heart watching its workings and taking record of every pulse" (p.228).

Her concern for Mr Rochester is shown as she cannot agree to the gipsy's suggestion of a happy marriage for him to Miss Ingram, and she tries to divert the conversation from more reference to him: "I did not come to hear Mr Rochester's fortune: I came to hear my own" (p.229). At this point it is possible that she might suspect something about the gipsy who seems to know so much about Mr Rochester, but she allows herself to be drawn in to the description of her face which is very thoughtful and accurate, especially about the conflict of feeling which has been shown frequently in Jane's response: "The passions may rage furiously, like true heathens ... but judgement shall still have the last word in every argument" (p.230).

After the 'gipsy' is revealed as Mr Rochester, he shows his admiration and need of Jane. The 'gipsy' is revealed as Mr Rochester himself when he becomes immersed in his commentary on Jane's nature and can no longer control his feelings for her: "I have acted as I inwardly swore I would act; but further might try me beyond my strength" (p.230). The realisation of Jane is carefully and realistically described; the confusion and uncertainty is suggested in her bewildered questions: "Where was I? Did I wake or sleep? Had I been dreaming? Did I dream still?" (p.231). The connection with a significant detail is another realistic aspect of someone gradually coming to recognition and having to convince himself of the truth: "... a broad ring flashed on the little finger, and stooping forward, I looked at it, and saw a gem I had seen a hundred times before" (p.231).

Jane's spirited personality is shown when she accuses Mr Rochester of not being fair with her; she is not immediately ready to forgive him his disguise: "I shall try to forgive you; but it was not right" (p.231). Probably Jane is disturbed that she may have let out some indiscreet comment on her feelings; Mr Rochester is sensitive to this as he reassures her: "Oh, you have been very correct — very careful, very sensible" (p.231). A renewal of the tone of respect and concern shown to Jane previously by Mr Rochester is almost established, deliberately so that the shock of hearing of Mr Mason's presence in the house is the more startling, as his grip on her wrist is "convulsive ... his lips froze ... a spasm caught his breath" (p.232). However, as the mutual understanding has been recalled, it is easier for the author to suggest further need for support for Mr Rochester being satisfied by Jane: "Jane, you offered me your shoulder once before; let me have it now"(p.232). She feels able to express her devotion directly now: "I'd give my life to serve you" (p.232).

Mr Rochester's solemn tone and urgent enquiries about the mood of the visitor and the other guests show how serious he considers Mr Mason's visit: "They don't look grave and mysterious, as if they had heard something strange?" (p.233); his questions to Jane about her constancy show his deep need of reassurance and comfort: "If all those people came in a body and spat at me, what would you do, Jane? ... if I were to go to them, and they only looked at me coldly ... and left me one by one, what then? Would you go with them?" (p.233). Jane's practical and commonsense reply is exactly appropriate to calm his fears: "I probably should know nothing about their ban; and if I did, I should care nothing about it" (p.233). The atmosphere changes again after the tension of this exchange; when Jane has taken the message to Mr Mason, she is reassured by the jovial tone of voice she hears after she has gone to bed; the chapter ends peacefully as she goes to sleep with "my heart at ease" (p.234).

Questions on Chapter Nineteen

1. How is Jane's distrust of the gipsy suggested in the first part of the chapter?
2. Which comments made by the gipsy seem to relate particularly to Jane's feelings for Mr Rochester?
3. What comments made by Jane show how she views the idea of a marriage between Mr Rochester and Miss Ingram?
4. How is Mr Rochester's vulnerability shown after he hears of Mr Mason?

Glossary

P.227 Communion: understanding, communication
P.227 Diablerie: devilry, evil
P.228 Moment: significance

Chapter Twenty

Summary

Jane is woken by a horrific scream and a struggle in the room above her. She waits for Mr Rochester to summon her, which he does when he has settled the disturbed household. Jane tends the visitor, Mr Mason, who has been attacked with a knife and bitten, Jane presumes, by Grace Poole. Mr Rochester fetches a surgeon to dress and bandage the wounds and meanwhile Jane stays with the man throughout the night. Mr Rochester is keen to get Mr Mason away from the house before the other guests are up and about, and insists on silence about the incident. Once Mr Mason has been driven away, Mr Rochester talks with Jane in the garden and explains how he wishes to rely on her strength and confidentiality, but he still does not explain the situation clearly and suggests he may marry Miss Ingram.

Commentary

A terrible scream is heard from the third storey of the house and the guests are all disturbed. When Mr Rochester has calmed them, he calls Jane to help him with Mr Mason, who has been wounded in a struggle, Jane believes, with Grace Poole. The chapter opens with an atmosphere of unease, a deliberate contrast with the sense of peace felt by Jane as she slept easily after her conversation with Mr Rochester. The moon is described as "beautiful, but too solemn", and the stark exclamation, "Good God! What a cry!" (p.235), is chilling in its effect. The violent imagery of the quiet of night torn apart by the sound is intensified by the harsh 's' sounds repeated in "a savage, a sharp, a shrilly sound ..." (p.235). As so often in this novel, the author involves the reader directly in the experience of the narrator by using physical description to explain emotional reaction; Jane recalls: "My pulse stopped; my heart stood still; my stretched arm was paralysed" (p.235).

This state of shocked rigidity is contrasted with the agitated activity of the roused household, skilfully suggested by the details of sounds, doors opening, people peeping out, eventually gathering in the gallery, and the constant questions: "'Oh! What is it?' — 'Who is hurt?' — 'What has happened?...'" (p.235). The exclamation marks, question marks and hyphens dramatise the excited, disturbed speech of the characters and increase the pace of the narrative. The dreadful sense of some terrible presence in the upper part of the house is increased by the reference to Mr Rochester having "just descended from the upper story" (p.236), linked with Jane's tracing the scream earlier to the third storey, and the sound of the struggle in the room above hers. Mr Rochester's explanations, though unsatisfactory to Jane, show his powerful persuasiveness; he is even able to calm the dowagers whom Jane somewhat sarcastically refers to as "bearing down on him like ships in full sail" (p.236).

A powerful sense of suspense is created as Jane waits in her room for some kind of summons; the references to "I knew not what ... some event ... hushed as a desert" (p.237), emphasise the mysterious mood; it is almost a relief for both narrator and reader when the knock comes at the door and at last Jane is taken to "the fateful third story" (p.237). Jane's practicality is shown when she has the required sponge and salts to hand and is calm enough to put a hand in Mr Rochester's that is "warm and steady" (p.238). The description of the room and the gradually revealed scene within is built up in carefully arranged stages, af first the sound of the snarling, then the laugh, which Jane still assumes to be that of Grace Poole, and then the ugly sight of Mason's side and arm, "almost soaked in blood" (p.238).

Jane stays with Mr Mason, bathing his wounds as instructed, until Mr Rochester returns with a surgeon. He is eager for Mr Mason to be gone and insists on silence between him and Jane, and about the incident. Mr Rochester's insistence on silence between Jane and the injured man he leaves her to tend further increases the mystery: "You will not speak to him on any pretext ... it will be at the peril of your life if you speak to her ... Remember! — no conversation ... these blue, still lips forbidden to unclose ..." (p.238-239). The tension and horror of Jane's lonely vigil by the wounded man is graphically described and her imaginative nature is once again made clear as she brings the characters of the apostles, carved on the cabinet panels, to life in her fearful thoughts. Naturally, her mind also ponders on the extraordinary situation she has become involved in, the continuous sequence of questions, from "What crime was this ..." to "Why *did* Mr Rochester enforce this concealment?" (p.239-240) effectively conveys the constant anxiety of Jane's bewilderment, developing into a desperate longing for his return: "'When will he come? When will he come?' I cried inwardly as the night lingered and lingered ..." (p.240).

Mr Rochester's nervousness and agitation on his return is shown in his brusque determination that his visitor is fit enough to leave; his insistence seems to be partly to reassure himself: "... it is nothing serious ... you've lost a little blood, that's all ..." (p.241). A more sinister impression of the attack Mr Mason has suffered is introduced when the surgeon fetched to attend to him notices "there have been teeth here!" (p.241). This links with the references to a snarling sound and the bestial description of the attacker: "She worried me like a tigress" (p.241) and the horrific comment, "She sucked the blood: she said she'd drain my heart" (p.242).

Despite these ghastly suggestions, Jane is still calm and practical, following all Mr Rochester's directions in fetching fresh clothes and Mr Mason's cloak; thus the author shows how she is keeping her vow to aid her employer in any way she can. Jane's dedication and dutiful responses show how dependable she is; despite the horror and mystery of the situation, she unquestioningly does as she is asked. When she has fetched the 'cordial' as instructed, the comments Mr Rochester makes about its origins, "... of an Italian charlatan — a fellow you would have kicked, Carter" (p.243), suggest an illegal drug and further the impression of a dark and mysterious past life in which Mr Rochester has made contact with a variety of unsavoury characters. Again, the urgency and determination of Mr Rochester in encouraging Mr Mason to leave show his anxiety to hide the events of the night from everyone else in the house; he only lets him sit "three minutes" after taking the 'cordial'; insists "I am sure you can get on your feet"; responds confidently, "I am sure you do" (p.243) to Mr Mason's suggestion that he feels better; and has the carriage waiting outside to dispatch him as hastily and noiselessly as possible.

The conversation between Mr Rochester and Mr Mason as he leaves shows concern for his welfare, as Mr Rochester plans to visit him and ensure that he does recover properly. As for the mysterious bestial woman who has made the attack, to Mason's plea, "Let her be taken care of: let her be treated as tenderly as may be; let her — ", Mr Rochester replies, "I do my best; and have done it, and will do it" (p.244). Clearly both men are compassionate and mutually supportive, and the terrible burden of the situation on Mr Rochester is shown when he lets his control slip slightly and exclaims, "Yet would to God there was an end of all this!" (p.244).

Mr Rochester confides in Jane about his feelings of desperation about a mistake he made earlier in his life, but does not explain fully exactly what he has done and what the consequences have been. His desperation colours the way he sees his home, as he describes it to Jane as being ugly and spoiled: "... the gilding is slime and the silk draperies cobwebs ... the polished woods mere refuse chips and scaly bark" (p.244). The harsh sounds of "slime ... cobwebs ... chips ... bark" emphasise the dreary melancholy of his mood which makes the beautiful house appear like this to him. In contrast, the beauty of the natural world outside calms him and he makes the first gentle and romantic gesture to Jane after all her dedication and support: "He gathered a half-blown rose, the first on the bush, and offered it to me" (p.245). His tender concern for her is revealed in his comments about leaving her alone during the night: "I should have been a careless shepherd if I had left a lamb — my pet lamb — so near a wolf's den, unguarded: you were safe". Jane has far more resilience and spirit than that suggested by the image of a lamb, but the idea of a desire to protect and care for an innocent is implied in Mr Rochester's description.

Jane is indeed innocent of the true attacker of Mr Mason and still supposes it to be Grace Poole, as shown in her fearful suggestion, typically more concerned for her employer than herself, "Yet it seems to me your life is hardly secure while she stays" (p.245). Jane's direct and honest approach also shows innocence in her response to Mr Rochester's vague hints of the risk of Mr Mason unintentionally destroying his happiness: "Tell him to be cautious, sir: let him know what you fear, and show him how to avert the danger" (p.245). Again, her trusting concern for him is very evident; she does not question what is causing the whole problem, to put her own mind at rest. Mr Rochester is shown to be taking advantage of Jane's trust and innocence to some extent; he does not enlighten her, but he is clearly affected by her virtuous nature and impressed by her sense of honour; he recognises that should he ask her to do anything that she considered wrong, "My friend would then turn to me, quiet and pale, and would say, "No, sir; that is impossible ..."" (p.246).

Mr Rochester's desire to confide in Jane and to have her under-standing of his circumstances is shown in his appeal to her in the garden, to sit with him as an equal rather than stand before him as his employee. The comments he makes about the natural activities of flowers, birds and bees suggest that he is hoping to persuade her that it was natural for him to act as he did, and that he should not be condemned. There is a suggestion also that he has been made aware of her imaginative nature, as he asks her to put herself in his place, "... imagine yourself in a remote foreign land; conceive that you there commit a capital error ..." (p.247). He is concerned about making it very clear to her that he has done nothing criminal: "not speaking of shedding of blood or any other guilty act" (p.247), and about showing how much he has suffered because of his mistake, through gloomy and despairing imagery, "your sun at noon darkens in an eclipse, which you feel will not leave it till the time of setting" (p.247). He still does not actually tell Jane what did happen to him, or what he did do to cause such distress and blight in his life, and the reader is as frustrated as the character; again the author skilfully involves the reader in the experience of her narrator.

When Mr Rochester refers to the desire "to attach to him for ever this gentle, gracious, genial stranger, thereby securing his own peace of mind and regeneration of life" (p.247), the author must intend the reader to hope that he means Jane herself is the person who will help him escape the bitter memories of his past life and give him new purpose; thus it is a carefully calculated shock to have him suggest that he would gain this through marriage to Miss Ingram. This is deliberately qualified, however, by the description of his changed tone and expression: "losing all its softness and gravity, and becoming harsh and sarcastic" (p.248), when he suggests this, thus he is still torn between the expectations of society and his own real desires, or between what he really wants and feels is right for him and the fear of harming Jane through the burden he might place on her through the relationship.

It seems strangely insensitive of Mr Rochester that he should ask Jane if she would sit with him the night before his marriage to Miss Ingram, as if perhaps he is testing the limits of her patience and dedication to him, yet she still responds positively, though in the briefest terms, "Yes, sir", as if she could not trust herself to say more without revealing her hurt. Tantalisingly the author does not give the reader any insight into her feelings at this point; the chapter ends very inconclusively with Jane's hearing Mr Rochester's cheerful covering up of the true events of the night, before his guests.

Questions on Chapter Twenty

1. How does the author create a sense of horror and disturbance in this chapter?
2. How is the relationship between Jane and Mr Rochester developed?
3. In what ways are the mystery of Thornfield and Mr Rochester's past increased in this chapter?
4. What further impression of Jane's nature and personality is given in this chapter?

Glossary

P.238 Pretext: reason, excuse
P.243 Charlatan: quack doctor
P.247 Conceive: imagine
P.247 Capital: punishable by death

Chapter Twenty-one

Summary

Jane has foreboding dreams and finds that Mrs Reed has been taken seriously ill and has sent for her. Jane returns to Gateshead and sits by her unpleasant aunt, prepared to be reconciled to her. John Reed has committed suicide and the shock has brought on a stroke; Eliza and Georgiana Reed are too selfish to care for their mother on her death bed.

Mrs Reed eventually admits to having received a letter from an uncle of Jane's three years previously and having replied to it, saying Jane had died of typhus at Lowood. This has prevented Jane from being adopted and cared for by the uncle, a John Eyre, living in Madeira. Mrs Reed dies without the comfort of any family beside her.

Commentary

Jane returns to Gateshead in response to a reluctant summons from the Reed sisters. The chapter opens suddenly, with an exclamation, "Presentiments are strange things!" (p.249) and the numerous references to dreams warning of trouble in both Bessie's and Jane's experience build up suspense in the reader until the connection is revealed by Jane receiving a visit from a servant "dressed in deep mourning" (p.249). This turns out to be Robert, from Gateshead, who married Bessie, and gradually the full reason for his coming is revealed. The author gives details sparingly and realistically, in the manner of someone breaking bad news, as Robert tells of John Reed's death, "... his life has been very wild ... His head was not strong ... — they say he killed himself" (p.250). Jane's natural kindness and lack of superiority over servants is shown in her warm greeting, using Robert's first name and directing him "to the care of John's wife and the attentions of John himself" (p.251). This is sharply contrasted with the attitude of Blanche Ingram to Jane, when she asks Mr Rochester for leave to attend her aunt; she "looked at me haughtily" and appears to see Jane as a "creeping creature", referring to her rudely as "that person" (p.251).

Mr Rochester's concern and care for Jane is suggested in his somewhat aggressive response to her request; he does not want her to go: "Nonsense, Jane! I would never think of running a hundred miles to see an old lady ..." (p.252). His reactions become almost pleading as he sees her resolve and the author skilfully shows how dear Jane has become to him by the strength of his opposition, "Promise me only to stay a week — ... you will not be induced under any pretext to take up a permanent residence with her?" (p.252). He is also concerned for her safety and wants to ensure that the coachman sent to accompany her is "a person to be trusted" (p.252). When he gives her money for the journey, he is brusque and slightly mocking, suggesting he is trying to hide his feelings of distress at her departure.

Jane is typically direct and honest in her response: "I told him I had no change ... I declined accepting more than was my due ... now you owe me five" (p.253). She is similarly direct and businesslike in her comments on the changes in the household she assumes will take place when Mr Rochester is married; again the author is showing how Jane too hides her feelings of dismay at the projected marriage to Blanche by her abruptness: "You have as good as informed me, sir, that you are going shortly to be married?" ... In that case, sir, Adele ought to go to school ... I must seek another situation somewhere" (p.253).

Mr Rochester's extreme reaction again shows his hardly contained feelings of distress: "... he exclaimed, with a twang of voice and a distortion of features equally fantastic and ludicrous ... 'At your peril you advertise!'" (p.253). The verbal battle between them continues as he asks for some of his money back and Jane refuses, again speaking bluntly and directly: "I could not spare the money on any account ... you are not to be trusted ... I'll promise you anything, sir, that I think I am likely to perform" (p.254). Her honesty and sense of duty are clear in her responses; when Mr Rochester attempts to draw some tenderness from her at their parting by implying she might take her leave in a less than formal way, she gives him no encouragement, denying herself the temptation of any belief in his fondness for her: "It is enough, sir: as much goodwill may be conveyed in one hearty word as in many" (p.254).

Jane reaches Gateshead and re-establishes her acquaintance with her aunt and cousins. When Jane reaches Gateshead, Bessie takes charge of her, much as she did when Jane was a child, and this leads to many comments by the author, through the narrator, on the contrast of Jane's situation in her past and present. The house is invested with a personality, just as it used to be in the young Jane's imagination: "On a dark, misty, raw morning in January, I had left a hostile roof ... The same hostile roof now again rose before me" (p.256). The emotions which caused Jane so much trouble are now calmed and she is no longer affected by the unpleasantness of her cousins: "The gaping wound of my wrongs ... was now quite healed" (p.256); "A sneer ... whether covert or open, had now no longer that power over me it once possessed" (p.257).

Jane's independence and social confidence are clearly evident as she no longer allows herself to be bullied or denied; when she is not taken to Mrs Reed, she goes to find Bessie to see if she can visit her aunt; when she goes up to her room "... to which I had often been summoned" (p.258), her actions are now described as active rather than passive: "I softly opened the door ... I approached the bed ... I opened the curtains ..." (p.258). The reader is taken with the narrator; the small details of Jane's approach create suspense until her aunt is clearly revealed, then another contrast is emphasised between Jane's former and present attitudes to the woman who had treated her so badly: "I had left this woman in bitterness and hate, and I came back to her now ... to be reconciled and clasp hands in amity" (p.259). In Mrs Reed, however, there is no change; she is as unforgiving as Jane is forgiving: "... resolved to consider me bad to the last ..." (p.259).

Jane's determination does not allow her to be disturbed by her aunt's coldness; her honesty admits to a longing to defeat the woman, "... to subdue her — to be her mistress ..." (p.259). It is as if the Jane Eyre who was herself subdued and mastered has disappeared, as Mrs Reed speaks of her as if she was not there, probably in her confused state: "I declare she talked to me once like something mad" (p.260). The author takes up the same impersonal tone in Jane's own responses, to suggest that the child she was has been replaced by the more confident and independent woman she has become: "... why do you hate her so?" (p.260).

The reader is at last given some more information about why Jane was treated so cruelly in her childhood; Mrs Reed's jealousy of her and her mother is revealed: "I had a dislike to her mother always; for she was my husband's only sister, and a great favourite with him ... he used to nurse it and notice it as if it had been his own: more indeed, than he ever noticed his own at that age" (p.260). The agitation and distress of Mrs Reed in her illness, and resentment, is shown in the frequent questions and exclamations as she explains this to Jane and as she thinks of her present situation: "What is to be done? How is the money to be had?" (p.261); she speaks as if her son were still alive and a trouble to her.

Jane learns of her cousins' lifestyles and preoccupations, hears of the letter from her uncle and recounts her aunt's death. The reader is kept in suspense, as Jane is, as to the reason why her aunt so wanted to see her. Jane whiles away her time sketching and the author shows her continual preoccupation with Mr Rochester as she draws his likeness, almost instinctively, as "... what sort of face it was to be, I did not care or know" (p.261). Once she has drawn it, however, she gains comfort merely from having her drawing of him to look at: "I smiled at the speaking likeness: I was absorbed and content" (p.262).

Neither of the daughters shows any care or concern for their mother; they are both selfish in their different ways. Georgiana "... favoured me with a description of the brilliant winter she had spent in London two seasons ago" (p.262), Eliza "divided her time into regular portions, and each hour had its alloted task" (p.263). Both refuse to consider reality and the problems in the family; each wants to get away and live the kind of life she wishes, Eliza in direct contrast to Georgiana, as she wants to "place safe barriers between herself and a frivolous world" (p.263). Their contrasting natures are nevertheless linked together by Jane's wry, pertinent observation that they both lacked any true humanity: "True, generous feeling is made small account by some; but here were two natures rendered, the one intolerably acrid, the other despicably savourless, for the want of it" (p.265). Once again the author uses a physical description, evoking a sense of taste, to skilfully describe an emotional effect and reaction.

Another descriptive feature frequently employed in this novel is the connection of weather and climate to the situations and circumstances of the characters; this is shown in the description of the wild and disturbed weather when Jane goes to her aunt's bedside again and learns of the letter from her uncle. It also reflects the turmoil suffered by Mrs Reed as she struggles with her conscience, knowing she is dying: "The rain beat strongly against the panes, the wind blew tempestuously ... that spirit — now struggling to quit its material tenement ..." (p.265).

The suspense is built up again as Jane's aunt asks her to assure her that they are alone in the room, then starts to tell her why she summoned her, then stops, and then eventually tells her to open the drawer and take out the letter and read it. The shock of the contents is made even more effective by having the letter written out on the page, rather than recounted in Jane's own words.

When Jane challenges her aunt over retaining her letter, her aunt's response typically blames Jane rather than herself: "I disliked you too fixedly ... I could not forget your conduct to me ... my last hour is racked by the recollection of a deed which, but for you, I should never have been tempted to commit" (p.267). Jane has clearly learned something from the selflessness of Helen Burns, of whom she thinks as she sees Mrs Reed is dying, for rather than denounce her for denying Jane the chance of a happier life under the protection of her uncle, she offers Mrs Reed the chance of redemption: "Many a time, as a little child, I should have been glad to love you if you would have let me: and I long earnestly to be reconciled to you now" (p.268). She feels "... only a grating anguish for *her* woes — not *my* loss ..." (p.268). The chapter ends on a very sombre note, as there has been none of her family with Mrs Reed as she died; the stark final sentence shows how little love or regret she had attracted: "Neither of us had dropped a tear" (p.268).

Questions on Chapter Twenty-one

1. Recount in your own words the feelings of Jane and Mr Rochester when she has to return to Gateshead. How does the author show that they are both trying to hide these feelings?
2. How are the contrasts between Jane as a child and Jane as a young woman shown in the chapter?
3. Comment on Jane's relationship with the two Reed sisters and their attitudes to each other and their mother, as shown in the chaper.
4. How is the deathbed revelation of Jane's uncle made dramatic?

Glossary

P.249 Presentiments: feelings of foreboding, warnings
P.252 Induced: persuaded
P.253 Twang: ring, nasal sound
P.253 Ludicrous: ridiculous
P.259 Reconciled: reunited
P.263 Frivolous: trivial
P.265 Acrid: bitter
P.265 Tenement: house
P.267 Racked: tortured

Chapter Twenty-two

Summary

Jane stays a month at Gateshead rather than the week she first intended, persuaded by first Georgiana and then Eliza to stay and help them. Eventually she returns to Thornfield in an uncertain mood, full of happiness yet questioning that happiness as caused by a man who she believes to be about to marry another woman.

Commentary

Jane patiently agrees to Georgiana's suggestion that she should stay on to help her and then does the same for Eliza. Eventually, after a month away, she returns to Thornfield. Georgina goes to live in London society; Eliza does the opposite and goes to a Roman Catholic convent in France. Jane makes her feelings clear, but only to herself in Georgiana's case, thinking that if she had to live with Georgiana longer, "I should assign you your share of labour, and compel you to accomplish it ..." (p.269). With Eliza she is more direct: "You are not without sense, cousin Eliza; but what you have, I suppose, in another year will be walled up alive in a French convent ... I don't much care" (p.270). Her rather cynical reaction to a life of contemplation is shown in what she does not say aloud, however: "'The vocation will fit you to a hair,' I thought: 'much good may it do you!'"(p.270). Jane has always been shown to have to rely on her self determination and resources of strength to keep herself; this retiring attitude of Eliza's clearly seems weak to her.

Her own lack of comfort and provision is emphasised as she sets out once again for Thornfield: "How people feel when they are returning home from an absence, long or short, I did not know: I had never experienced the sensation" (p.270). This reference to home is to be significantly repeated in her conversation with Mr Rochester once she does return.

The swings of mood Jane experiences as she makes her way back are realistically expressed and the uncertainty regarding Mr Rochester's proposed marriage are well prepared for. In Jane's letter from Mrs Fairfax "she said the idea of his marrying Miss Ingram still seemed strange to her" (p.271); the weather seems to reflect a positive mood as "the sky, though far from cloudless, was such as promised well for the future" (p.271), but the reference to clouds suggests problems to encounter; Jane is confused as "I stopped once to ask myself what that joy meant" and she tries to convince herself: "he is not thinking of you" (p.271).

Jane returns to Thornfield and finds Mr Rochester sitting outside; her confused and uncertain feelings for him and his responses to her result in her most direct acknowledgement of her true feelings towards him. Jane's approach to the house is made very vivid by the use of the present tense, as if it is actually happening now, "I arrive ... I have no time ... I see the narrow stile ... I see — Mr Rochester sitting there ..." (p.272). The tension mounts through the stages carefully depicted as she gets nearer and nearer and the tension in Jane is shown in a powerful description: "... every nerve I have is unstrung ...". She has an unnerving sensation, as she is usually so well in control of herself, "... for a moment I am beyond my own mastery" (p.272). The skilful description continues when Jane is spotted by Mr Rochester; again the present tense and the idea of an uncontrolled response is used: "I suppose I do come on, though in what fashion I know not; being scarcely cognizant of my movements" (p.272).

The confusion created both in reader and narrator is continued as Jane fiercely reminds herself, "... he was so soon to cease to be my master" (p.273), yet Mr Rochester is tender towards her, smiling with "the real sunshine of feeling"; using a diminutive of her name:

"Pass, Janet"; suggesting she is family: "go up home ..."; and using gentle encouragement: "... stay your weary little wandering feet at a friend's threshold." (p.273).

His use of the term "home" creates a surge of longing in her and she can no longer hold back her feelings, admitting, in her further repetition of the word, " ... wherever you are is my home — my only home" (p.274). This admission is not rejected, yet again there is reference to her insistence on not assuming that she is really wanted, "... the voice that kept warning me of near separation and coming grief" (p.274). This is further confused by the comments that "nothing was said of the master's marriage ... there was no journeying backward and forward, no visits to Ingram Park" (p.274), and finally, at the end of the chapter, the contrasting sense of despair and joy in the exasperated admission: "alas! never had I loved him so well" (p.275).

Questions on Chapter Twenty-two

1. How are the contrasting personalities of Jane, Eliza and Georgiana shown in the first part of the chapter?
2. How are Jane's confused feelings conveyed to the reader in the later part of the chapter?

Glossary

P.269 Assign: give, allot
P.269 Compel: force

Chapter Twenty-three

Summary

Jane goes out into the orchard in the fading heat of midsummer; she is joined by Mr Rochester who discusses various details of the household situation as if he is to be shortly married to Miss Ingram. He is torn between the society match he might make and the true marriage he really wants with Jane. He talks the whole situation through with her, testing her reaction to find that she really does love him; he then astonishes her by proposing marriage to her, and she accepts him.

Commentary

Mr Rochester tests Jane's feelings for him as he talks with her in the garden. The opening mood of the chapter is full of happiness and the suggestion of fulfilment, created through the description of light and warmth, "midsummer shone ... suns so radiant ... sunny hue" (p.276) and nature mellow and ripe, "trees in their dark prime ... full-leaved ... trees laden with ripening fruit ... fruit, large as plums ... a ripe cherry ..." (p.276-277). The sensuous nature of the language of this chapter continues with many descriptions of vivid colour: "... roads white ... a solemn purple ... red jewel ... fine, deep blue ..." (p.276).

The emphasis on the senses is developed still further with the reference to the smell of Mr Rochester's cigar smoke and this acts as a warning sign to Jane that she is not alone, as she would wish, in the orchard. The ripeness of nature is used in the description by the author to suggest the ripeness of the relationship between Jane and Mr Rochester; they are ready to take this step further, but the

114

teasing tone and apparently deliberately confusing approach taken by Mr Rochester undermines this. The teasing approach is first suggested as Jane tries to get out of the garden and he pretends not to have noticed her, before suddenly suggesting she looks at the moth he seems to have been studying. A slight warning note is sounded in his reference to it seeming like a "West Indian insect" (p.277) , reminding Jane and the reader of his mysterious past.

Mr Rochester continues with the misleading conversation he had with Jane on her return, about his prospective marriage, reminding her of her own suggestions before she left for Gateshead that she would have to look for other employment and Adele would have to go to school. He does not ever precisely say he is to marry Miss Ingram, but he refers to rumour having suggested it, perhaps thus giving a hint that it is not so. He takes Jane in, however, and just says very vaguely, "In about a month I hope to be a bridegroom" (p.279).

He is deliberately pressing her to declare her true feelings and does this in what seems a somewhat cruel way, suggesting a family to which Jane might go to work as governess in Ireland. It is at this suggestion that the author shows Jane's resolve to control herself breaking; she refers to the distance and the sea as "a barrier ... From England and Thornfield: and — ... From *you,* sir" (p.279). The short phrases and frequent punctuation show the agitation which is expressed as Jane makes this admission. The names chosen by Mr Rochester for the probably imaginary family should be seen as indicating the distaste which he really feels for this suggestion: "Mrs O'Gall of Bitternut Lodge" implying a bitter experience, but this is not noticed at first reading or when Jane hears the suggestion from the man she loves and wants to stay near.

After further apparently contradictory remarks, Mr Rochester proposes to Jane. She is absolutely astonished, but does accept him. Mr Rochester makes further comments which seem to be definitely concluding that he is not to see Jane again: "... we will sit there in peace tonight, though we should never more be destined to sit there together" (p.280), but then he talks of "... if I can't do better" than send Jane away and speaks of being metaphorically joined to her, "tightly and inextricably knotted" and of the wound he would suffer if they were parted, "I should take to bleeding inwardly ..." (p.280). Jane is very disturbed by these conflicting remarks and the dread of losing her contact with him; as so often, her emotional turmoil is powerfully expressed in physical terms, "I was shaken from head to foot with acute distress" (p.280).

Jane is forced to acknowledge what she really loves about her relationship with Mr Rochester: "I have talked, face to face, with what I reverence, with what I delight in — with an original, a vigorous, an expanded mind" (p.281). When he agrees he will have a bride — again not exactly specifying that it will be Blanche — and yet also says Jane must not go, this is too much to take. Jane at last breaks into a passionate statement of her sense of self worth, "Do you think, because I am poor, obscure, plain, and little, I am soulless and heartless? You think wrong! ... it is my spirit that addresses your spirit ... equal as we are!" This brave and splendid speech is clearly more than the words of a created character; the author's intense feeling for women's needs for recognition as intellectual and social equals with men is surely expressed here.

It is this declaration of heartfelt unity which really moves Mr Rochester to claim the happiness of both himself and Jane, yet at his delight in taking her to him in an embrace, a negative note is sounded as Jane, most ironically, says, "... you are a married man ..." (p.281). Of course she goes on to say, "— or as good as a married man" (p.282), and she clearly means to Blanche Ingram, but the protest is very ironic in the light of later events. Jane is still convinced that Mr Rochester intends to marry Miss Ingram, and when he offers her his possessions and companionship she assumes he is cruelly taunting her: "You play a farce. which I merely laugh at" (p.282).

Naturally, even when he directly and clearly states his real intentions and desires, Jane cannot take it in and is dumbstruck; the description is extremely realistic: "Still I did not answer, and still I writhed myself from his grasp: for I was still incredulous" (p.282).

Jane's directness and honesty are shown again in her spirited response to his questions; the short sentences show the tension between them in this exchange:

"Do you doubt me, Jane?"

"Entirely."

"You have no faith in me?"

"Not a whit."

When she is eventually persuaded, it is terms of truth, honour and virtue that she responds: "If you are true, and your offer real ... Are you in earnest? Do you truly love me? Do you sincerely wish me to be your wife?" (p.283). Once again the author creates a direct contrast with the happiness as Jane wonderingly accepts the proposal, again through a very ironic remark of Jane's: "There is no one to meddle, sir. I have no kindred to interfere" (p.284).

Mr Rochester's apparently meaningless and dark mutterings show how he desperately wants this proposed marriage to remain unhindered, and he tries to persuade himself that a good relationship now will wipe out the legacy of a less suitable one earlier in his life: "It will atone — it will atone ... It will expiate at God's tribunal ... For man's opinion — I defy it" (p.284). The weather is deliberately linked once again with the situation, as the balmy summer evening changes into a violently stormy night, heralding the storms and disruption to come in the relationship, "But what had befallen the night? The moon was not yet set, and we were all in shadow ... what ailed the chestnut tree? it writhed and groaned ... there was a crack, a crash, and a close rattling peal ..." (p.284). To underline even further the ominous note of the end of the chapter, as they return to the house, "the clock was on the stroke of twelve", midnight being referred to as the witching hour, and in the morning the suggestion that Jane and Rochester are to be split apart even as they seem to have found happiness together is foreshadowed in the report by Adele that "... the great horse-chestnut at the bottom of the orchard had been struck by lightning in the night, and half of it split away" (p.285).

Questions on Chapter Twenty-three

1. What part does the weather play in the emphasis of mood in this chapter?
2. How does Mr Rochester confuse and upset Jane when talking with her in the garden?
3. Show how successfully the author describes human emotions in this chapter.

Glossary

P.280 Inextricably: intricately, inescapably
P.282 Incredulous: disbelieving
P.284 Atone: make up, repair
P.284 Expiate: make amends

Chapter Twenty-four

Summary

Rochester's and Jane's ideas of courtship are seen to be widely different. He has a romanticised view of her as his bride; she does not want to be changed from her real self. She refuses to change their behaviour towards each other during the day at Thornfield; after Mrs Fairfax's warnings to be careful, Jane devises various means to keep herself separate from him except in the evenings.

Commentary

Jane feels happy but uncertain about Mr Rochester's courtship of her; she tries to counteract his exaggerated delight and finds some of his attentions patronising. The effect of mutual love on Jane is to make her look more attractive; her confidence in herself is increased by her knowledge of Mr Rochester's true love for her: "I was sure I might lift my face to his now and not cool his affection by its expression" (p.286). Once again the mood of the characters is reflected in the weather: the stormy night has changed again to a bright, fresh day, as Jane remarks, "Nature must be gladsome when I was so happy" (p.286).

Jane's comments on Mr Rochester's endearments are gently teasing, especially about his describing her green eyes as hazel. The direct address to the reader is not often used but emphasises the slight distance the character maintains from her situation now she has regained control over herself. There is a slightly sinister note in Jane's comment on her reaction to Mr Rochester's referring to her name becoming Jane Rochester: "The feeling the announcement sent through me was something stronger than was consistent with

119

joy — something that smote and stunned: it was, I think, almost fear" (p.287). The underlying uncertainty is further emphasised in Jane's inability to really believe in herself as the future bride of Mr Rochester. This might be natural for someone in her situation, especially after the strange way in which he eventually proposed, but the reaction seems stronger than just a happy daze, "... it does not sound likely. Human beings never enjoy complete happiness in this world" (p.287).

The difficulties Jane would have in adjusting to the social implications of the marriage are suggested in her reaction to his offer of rich jewels and fine clothing, "Jewels for Jane Eyre sounds unnatural and strange: I would rather not have them ... I shall not be your Jane Eyre any longer but an ape in a harlequin's jacket — a jay in borrowed plumes" (p.287,288). Jane's down-to-earth and commonsense attitude warns against Mr Rochester trying to make her something she is not; her sense of self-worth and her independence insist on her being valued as she is: "I will be myself. Mr Rochester, you must neither expect nor exact anything celestial of me — for you will not get it, any more than I shall get it of you ..." (p.288). It is likely that Jane is protecting herself as she used to do as a child, from possible disappointment, by foreseeing it, as she retorts to Mr Rochester's insistence on his constancy: "I wonder how you will answer me a year hence, should I ask a favour it does not suit your convenience or pleasure to grant" (p.289).

A sense of tension and uneasiness is suggested when Jane refers to her curiosity; clearly Mr Rochester has much to hide, as an innocent question about Miss Ingram provokes extreme relief that she had not wanted to know about anything else: "Is that all? Thank God it is no worse!" (p.291). Jane clearly states her desire for directness and honesty in her husband to match her own as she suggests the pretence of wishing to marry Blanche was underhand and cruel: "It was a burning shame and a scandalous disgrace to act in that way" (p.291). Further uneasiness is suggested at Mrs

Fairfax's reaction to the news of Mr Rochester's intention to marry Jane. She has to make "a sort of effort to smile, and framed a few words of congratulation; but the smile expired, and the sentence was abandoned unfinished" (p.292). Later in their conversation she confirms her concern regarding the relationship with vague and unnerving comments: "I do fear there will be something found to be different to what either you or I expect ... believe me, you cannot be too careful" (pp.293,294). Such remarks seem more than just surprise or uncertainty at the age gap or social distance of the two; again the author is subtly preparing the reader for later developments in the story.

Mr Rochester's extravagance becomes embarassing and even humiliating for Jane. She insists on trying to maintain their relationship as governess and employer until they are actually married. Mr Rochester's harsher side is shown in his reaction to Jane's suggestion that Adele should accompany them to Millcote: "I'll have no brats!" (p.294), although he eventually relents. The imaginative idea of taking Jane to the moon which he tells the child is rejected in practical and suggestive terms: "She will have nothing to eat: you will starve her ... she will want to warm herself: what will she do for a fire? ... But you can't get her there; there is no road to the moon ..." (p.295). The objections could be seen as reflecting the romanticised and impractical aspects of Mr Rochester's view of marriage to Jane. This is developed through his choice of dresses for her, so totally different from what she is used to wearing. Jane shows a stubborn streak in refusing them and eventually accepting two very plain grey and black dresses instead of half a dozen in glorious colours; again their differences in personality and style reflect deeper contrasts which might cause disruption in a marriage. Jane feels the humiliation of being a kept woman rather than a poor but independent individual, as though she herself is being bought: "... the more he bought me, the more my cheek burned with a sense of annoyance and degradation" (p.297).

Mr Rochester seems to become patronising once he feels he has Jane as his prospective bride, another difficulty to create potential problems: "Is she piquant? I would not exchange this one little English girl for the Grand Turk's whole seraglio ..." (p.297). His use of descriptions of the Eastern Harem insults Jane and also recalls again the exotic travels of the past which have affected his life and about which Jane knows nothing. Jane's pride is shown in further rejection of the favours and attentions Mr Rochester hopes to give her; her determination and stubbornness is taken to extremes as she takes to heart what Mrs Fairfax has suggested and says she sees no reason to dine with him "till I can't help it" and "shall keep out of your way all day as I have been accustomed to do" (pp. 298-299).

Jane's detachment is extraordinary, as she works out ways in which to keep the man she loves from any kind of intimacy with her, devising plans to keep him occupied. Even her delight in his fine singing voice is tempered by a fear of unwisely flattering him, "I was not fond of pampering that susceptible vanity of his; but for once, and from motives of expediency, I would e'en soothe and stimulate it" (p.299). The song Mr Rochester sings is clearly deliberately chosen to reflect the situation between himself and Jane; the reference to rejecting possible retribution is another hint of difficulties to come; he is singing a temptation to providence! "I care not in this moment sweet/ Though all I have rushed o'er/ Should come on pinion, strong and fleet,/Proclaiming vengeance sore" (p.300). The disagreements over his treatment of her are expressed in slightly teasing terms, thus suggesting the familiarity of closeness enabling them to enter into such arguments; however, they also continue to suggest differences between them which could prove unsettling, and Jane is determined to ensure as far as possible that all potential difficulties are acknowledged before their wedding: "... he should know fully what sort of a bargain he had made, while there was yet time to rescind it" (p.301).

The fact that to some extent Jane and Mr Rochester are playing a game together in these weeks before their marriage, is suggested in Jane's calculating terms to describe their relationship: "The system thus entered on, I pursued during the whole season of probation ... Mrs Fairfax, I saw, approved me: her anxiety on my account vanished ..." (p.302). It is however, a serious game; Jane does not find it easy: "Often I would rather have pleased than teased him".

Questions on Chapter Twenty-four

1. What details in this chapter show differences in outlook and attitude between Jane and Rochester?
2. What is the importance of Mrs Fairfax and Adele in this chapter?
3. Where in this chapter does Jane show her pride and independent spirit?

Glossary

P.312 Hypothesis: supposition, suggested explanation

Chapter Twenty-five

Summary

Jane is very restless and agitated on the day before her wedding and superstitious about using her married name. She is most concerned to see Mr Rochester who has gone out, to tell him about an incident which has disturbed her terribly the previous night. When he returns, she tells him of her troubled dreams and of a terrifying visit from a horrifyingly ugly woman who tore Jane's wedding veil in two during the night. She is sure it is someone different from Grace Poole, who she has been led to believe causes the strange sounds she has heard previously. Mr Rochester attempts to calm and reassure her, but Jane is not convinced and passes a sleepless and troubled night before her wedding day.

Commentary

Jane is tense and unhappy; she looks through her wedding clothes ready for the following day, goes out to the orchard to see the tree struck in the storm and anxiously awaits Mr Rochester's return. Jane still seems very nervous and uncertain about her forthcoming marriage to Mr Rochester; rather than eager expectation, it is almost with dread that she awaits the day: "There was no putting off the day that advanced — the bridal day" (p.303). She is superstitious about fixing on the labels with her married name to her luggage before she is actually Mrs Rochester: "I would wait to be assured she had come into the world alive before I assigned to her all that property" (p.303). Even her wedding dress seems more like a ghost's clothing; Jane refers to it as "wraith-like ... ghostly ... white dream" (p.303), all suggesting that there will be complications, that the idea of the wedding is as unreal and insubstantial as a dream or a ghostly vision. These supernatural images create an eerie and tense atmosphere in the opening of the chapter.

The author uses the direct address of Jane to the reader to add yet more suspense, about an incident which happened the previous night, which she wants to talk to Mr Rochester about: "Stay till he comes, reader; and, when I disclose my secret to him, you shall share the confidence" (p.304). As so often in the novel, the weather is described as reflecting the characters' feelings and situation; the disturbed and uncertain mood is expressed through the wildness of the wind, which "seemed to augment its rush and deepen its roar" (p.304).

Jane goes to the orchard to look at the damaged tree and the fact that it has not completely split suggests that despite difficulties, Jane and Mr Rochester will not be completely separated, but will be always connected despite partings, like two parts of the tree, "for the firm base and strong roots kept them unsundered below" (p.304). Jane wanders around, in and out of the house, impatient for Mr Rochester to return. The increase of bad weather reflects her distress: "... the night grew dark; rain came driving fast on the gale" (p.305).

When Mr Rochester comes back, he is disturbed by Jane's mood; she eventually tells him of her dreams and the horrifying night visit. Mr Rochester's concern at Jane's agitation and her coming out to meet him when he does eventually return, shows his tenderness towards her; his anxious enquiries: "Is there anything wrong? ... is there anything the matter?" (p.306) and her vague reference to having been afraid and unhappy in his absence add to the sense of mystery and tension developed from the beginning of the chapter. The same sense of unreality and nervous apprehension about the wedding are emphasised as she says even he is "... the most phantom-like of all ..." (p.307).

When Mr Rochester starts to outline the arrangements for the following day, after the wedding, Jane's reaction is strange and disturbing; she is clearly agitated: "What a bright spot of colour you have on each cheek! and how strangely your eyes glitter!" (p.307). Clearly she is very troubled and Mr Rochester's anxious questions only have vague responses from her. The author is keeping the reader in suspense, for even when Jane starts to explain why she feels so unsettled, it is a long, detailed story of her feelings and actions during the previous day. She recalls the change of spirits in herself reflected in the weather: "I wondered why moralists call this world a dreary wilderness: for me it blossomed like a rose. Just at sunset, the air turned cold and the sky cloudy ..." (p.308). Then she recounts finding the extravagant, jewelled veil Mr Rochester has left with her wedding dress, and shows as in previous incidents how differently she feels about herself, feeling she only needs "... the square of unembroidered blond I had myself prepared as a covering for my low-born head" (p.308).

She has still not revealed what actually disturbed her so much, and the eerie suspense continues with her references to the wild wind and the mournful sounds of the gale. She mentions a dream of a child she has as she first slept; this recalls her earlier comments about overhearing Bessie say that dreams of children usually forewarned trouble. Mr Rochester's attempts at calming her with words of love do not change her mood and the reader is drawn even further into the supernatural world of dreams as Jane tells of another, even more fearful dream, "... that Thornfield Hall was a dreary ruin ... you were departing for many years ... the wall crumbled; I was shaken; the child rolled from my knee ..." (p.310). The child is symbolic of the love for Rochester that Jane must protect at all costs, denied by threats and challenged by consequences of Mr Rochester's past life, soon to be revealed. The dream is clearly meant as a warning of events which will happen before Jane and Rochester can finally be properly united.

Eventually Jane tells of the most horrific incident in her 'dream', the appearance of the strange woman who tore her veil. This 'dream' is clearly an actual event, and is vividly and hauntingly described. The realisation that the figure is no-one she knows is skilfully recalled by the typical technique of physical description of emotional response: "... my blood crept cold through my veins", and the repetition of negatives: "... this was not Sophie, it was not Leah, it was not Mrs Fairfax ... it was not even that strange woman, Grace Poole" (p.311).

The ghastly description of the distorted face of the madwoman who came into Jane's room is powerfully expressed by repetition of "fearful", and the dark, ugly colours, "red eyes ... blackened inflation ... purple ... black eyebrows ... bloodshot eyes ..." (p.311). The horror of the recollection is brought to a frightening climax as Jane describes the horrific figure coming over to her and putting out the candle after holding it to her face. She links the terrifying incident with the time she fainted before, after she had been locked up in the red room at Gateshead as a child: "... for the second time in my life — only the second time — I became insensible from terror" (p.312).

When Mr Rochester tries to calm Jane, he does not offer any other explanation apart from insisting that the strange woman must have been Grace Poole. Jane is not reassured and sleeps in the nursery rather than her own room for her last night before her wedding. Mr Rochester's attempts to reassure Jane that the events of the night are only in her mind only increase the sense of dread and tension, as when he questions her as to whether such things as she dreamed have happened, she can only reply "Not yet" (p.312). The dramatic power of this part of the chapter is increased yet again when Jane reveals that the veil had actually been torn. The use of hyphens to create dramatic pauses in her speech emphasises the horror of the realisation: "... there — on the carpet — I saw what gave the distinct lie to my hypothesis – the veil, torn from top to bottom ..." (p.312). The 'hypothesis', the proposed suggestion, that all was well, was destroyed by this sight, as is Mr Rochester's calm mood: "I felt Mr Rochester start and shudder ... He drew his breath short, and strained me so close to him ..." (p.312).

Clearly Mr Rochester is deeply disturbed by the situation Jane has described, yet he does not attempt to explain it, thus again the reader is kept in suspense. He continues "cheerily" to talk to Jane and suggests the strange visitor must have been Grace Poole after all. He tries to put her at ease but only makes the atmosphere more tense by suggesting there is some further explanation he could give but he wants to have Jane definitely his wife before he will reveal anything else about the woman he still insists is Grace Poole: "... when we have been married a year and a day, I will tell you; but not now" (p.313). Jane's uncertainty and the lack of full communication between herself and her intended husband is shown in her hiding her true feelings: "... satisfied I was not, but to please him I endeavoured to appear so" (p.313).

The unspoken concern and dread of Mr Rochester is suggested as he insists that Jane go to sleep with Adele in the nursery and bolt the door; although the weather now seems to be calm, the wind has changed from roaring to "soft whispers" (p.313); the underlying mood of the last part of the chapter is still tense as Jane does not sleep at all. The night before her wedding is a stressful and troubled one, as she nurses Adele in her arms. The end of the chapter is full of foreboding, as Jane refers to Adele as a symbol of her own past life; she is entering on another stage of her journey of development and the security she has built up will be shattered. The reference to Mr Rochester as "dread" and "adored" (p.314), further emphasises Jane's mixed emotions and uncertainty as she approaches her marriage.

Questions on Chapter Twenty-five

1. What details does the author give to show how nervous and uncertain Jane is in this chapter?
2. How is the reader kept in suspense during this chapter?
3. Give examples of vivid description of character and setting which add to the drama of this part of the novel.
4. Show how the supernatural plays an important part in this stage of Jane's story.

Glossary

P.303 Assigned: allocated, gave
P.308 Blond: plain cloth
P.312 Hypothesis: supposition, suggested explanation

Chapter Twenty-six

Summary

Jane and Rochester's wedding is dramatically stopped as a stranger, revealed as Mr Mason's solicitor, enters the church with Mr Mason and reveals that Mr Rochester had previously been married. His wife, Bertha, is Mr Mason's sister and is living in Thornfield Hall under guard.

Commentary

Mr Rochester is extremely eager to complete the wedding ceremony; Jane has a sense of foreboding and uncertainty. The chapter opens with a sense of haste and impatience on Mr Rochester's part, as if he wants the ceremony over as quickly as possible so that he can really claim Jane as his own. He "... sent up to ask why I did not come ... 'Lingerer!' he said ... he would give me about ten minutes to eat some breakfast ... it must be ready the moment we return ..." (p.315). The lack of guests or supporters for the ceremony and the determined resolution of Mr Rochester make the last few minutes before the marriage strained and tense; the suggestions of disturbance in the bridegroom create a feeling of foreboding: his "flaming and flashing eyes" and "the thoughts whose force he seemed breasting and resisting" (p.316).

The gloomy graves and headstones and the presence of two strangers who slip into the church unnerve Jane and she has a further feeling of premonition, though not consciously acknowledged, when "I felt my forehead dewy, and my cheeks and lips cold". The frequently noted technique of the author in describing mental and emotional states in physical terms is once again evident here. The dramatic revelation which stops the ceremony is skilfully prepared for in the charting of the progress of the strangers, first seen in the graveyard, then ahead of the bride and groom in the church, then one of them "advancing up the chapel" (p.316).

Mr Mason's solicitor stops the wedding by announcing an impediment: Mr Rochester's previous wife is still living. The traditional words of the wedding service are wound into the narrative of the chapter and the comment of the central character herself makes the reader very conscious of impending disruption: "When is the pause after that sentence ever broken by reply? Not perhaps, once in a hundred years" (p.317). When the stranger announces "I declare the existence of an impediment" (p.317), it is the culmination of hints and suggestions in several previous chapters; the reader is invited to connect so many little details of Jane's reluctance and nervousness, Mr Rochester's uneasiness, the strange sounds and visitations at Thornfield, and this makes the simple words charged with dreadful power.

The reaction of Mr Rochester is effectively conveyed as he tries to deny the awful challenge, attempting to ignore the interruption and refuse to acknowledge that what he feared has happened: "... taking a firmer footing, and not turning his head or eyes, he said, 'Proceed' ... he stood stubborn and rigid ..." (p.317). The explanation by the stranger of his declaration is made dramatic by the variety of adverbs preparing for the actual words themselves, adding to the suspense of the moment: "... uttering each word distinctly, calmly, steadily, but not loudly " (p.317).

Jane's reaction to the news of Mr Rochester's wife's existence is rigidly controlled, yet shown to be shattering, especially in terms of the unnatural aspect of the situation, contrasted with a reaction to natural extremes: "My nerves vibrated to those low-spoken words as they had never vibrated to thunder — my blood felt their subtle violence as it had never felt frost or fire" (p.318). The repetition of the negative, "never", makes the understated description more dramatic, for so often the author describes weather and other natural features as in sympathy with the character's feelings, reflecting the situation in the human world.

The solicitor's reading of the official statement of Mr Rochester's previous marriage and the presentation of Mr Mason in the church are described in a very straightforward way. The lack of elaborate language enhances the dramatic tension which culminates in Mr Rochester's near-attack on Mason, vividly described as the emotion surges through his body and is suddenly dissipated: "... his face flushed — olive cheeks and hueless forehead received a glow as from spreading ascending heart-fire ... his passion died as if a blight had shrivelled it up ..." (p.319).

Mr Rochester leads Jane and the others up to the third storey of Thornfield to see the madwoman he was earlier tricked into marrying. Once Mr Rochester realises that his dream of another, happier marriage is impossible, he is resolved to reveal everything, and the language takes on a determined and resolute tone: "Enough! all shall bolt out at once, like the bullet from the barrel ... there will be no wedding to-day" (p.319). The suffering he has been through is made clear in his following explanation of the circumstances surrounding the first marriage: "You shall see what sort of a being I was cheated into espousing, and judge whether or not I had a right to break the compact, and seek sympathy with something at least human" (p.320). The reader is drawn to sympathy with him whilst also being made aware of the links between the various strange events attributed to Grace Poole in earlier chapters. As in other stages of the novel, the reader shares the experience with the central character; Jane is at last made aware of the reason for the mystery surrounding her intended husband's past.

The stages by which the group of people reach the upper storey of the house are described in some detail, then the features of the room in which the mad Bertha Mason is kept; this creates further suspense until the final description of the frightening figure, the same as that which had entered Jane's room and split her veil: "The maniac bellowed: she parted her shaggy locks from her visage and gazed wildly at her visitors. I recognised well that purple face — those bloated features" (p.321). The details of the revelation are given without any reference to how Jane feels, implying that she is numbed by the shock of events and the disastrous cancellation of the marriage.

The violence and ugliness of the madness which has possessed Bertha is dramatically emphasised by the physicality of the language used to describe her attack on Mr Rochester: "... the lunatic sprang and grappled ... struggled ... virile force ... athletic ... wrestle ... convulsive plunges" (pp.321-322). Mr Rochester's bitterness at his loss of hope for a happier life is shown in his contrast of Bertha with Jane and his sarcastic reference to that which he has to accept: "I must shut up my prize" (p.322). The skill with which the author links coincidental connections in the narrative is shown when it is revealed by the solicitor that Jane's uncle knew Mr Mason and alerted him to the situation when he received Jane's letter about her prospective marriage; "He could not then hasten to England himself, to extricate you from the snare into which you had fallen ..." (p.322).

Jane's reactions to the distressing events are described. At last the reader is given some indication of Jane's feelings about the traumatic events she has experienced, when she explains her sense of unreality and strange detachment once back in her own room: "... till now I had only heard, seen, moved — followed up and down where I was led or dragged — watched event rushed on event ..." (p.323). She has been too bewildered and shocked to respond directly, mesmerised by the awful situation; only when alone can she think about all that has happened. The difficulty of taking it in, fully comprehending what the situation means for her, is skilfully conveyed in the feeling of unreality and disbelief that outwardly and personally nothing has changed, yet nothing can ever be the same:

"... nothing had smitten me, or scathed me, or maimed me. And yet where was the Jane Eyre of yesterday? — where was her life? — where were her prospects?" (p.323).

The images from the book Jane had read as a child at Gateshead which then reflected her desolate state, and the dream symbol of the vulnerable child representing her love, are both recalled in the natural descriptions of her spoiled hopes: "A Christmas frost had come at midsummer ... waste, wild, and white as pine-forests in wintry Norway ... a suffering child in a cold cradle ..." (pp.323-324). The chapter ends with dramatic imagery of drowning, as the full implications of the thwarted marriage come over Jane and she realises she will have to leave Thornfield and the only real happiness and security she has known are destroyed: "... a flood loosened ... I felt the torrent come ... the torrent poured over me ... the floods overflowed me" (p.324).

Questions on Chapter Twenty-six

1. How does the author create a dramatic atmosphere in this chapter?
2. Describe Jane's feelings before and after the disruption of the wedding ceremony.
3. Which threads of plot are linked up in this chapter, and what mysteries are explained?

Glossary

P.317 Rigid: hard, stiff
P.319 Blight: plant disease
P.320 Espousing: marrying
P.320 Compact: arrangement, legal agreement

P.321 Visage: face
P.321 Bloated: swollen, distorted
P.321 Virile: powerful
P.322 Convulsive: violently jerky
P.322 Extricate: release, deliver
P.323 Maimed: crippled, disabled

Chapter Twenty-seven

Summary

Jane wrestles with her conscience which tells her she must leave Rochester and Thornfield. Rochester tries to persuade her to stay as his wife, and attempts to explain why he does not consider himself bound by his first marriage. He tells the long, detailed story of the circumstances surrounding his being tricked into marriage with Bertha Mason and his life since then, including his delight at meeting Jane. Jane has a terrible struggle between her desire to stay with Rochester and her duty to reject an unlawful relationship, and eventually she drags herself away and leaves the house very early in the morning to take a coach to a far-off place.

Commentary

Jane stays in her room to try to recover her strength after the shock of the disallowed marriage; Mr Rochester tries to find out how Jane feels, and to explain everything. The opening of the chapter gives a graphic account of the turmoil in Jane's mind as she considers the prospect of leaving Thornfield and resists it. Her old struggle between duty and desire is reawakened and the personification of the two aspects of her nature as Conscience and Passion dramatises her fear of the consequences of giving in to her longing to stay: "... he would thrust her down to unsounded depths of agony" (p.325). Mr Rochester's concern for Jane is shown as he has let her take her time to adjust to her distress, yet has waited outside her door in case she needed his help, despite her thinking he and others of the household has deserted her: "... five minutes more of that deathlike hush, and I should have forced the lock like a burglar" (p.326).

His desperate regret at hurting her is shown to be genuine in his expectation of her reproach of him and Jane's own unchanged love for him is made clear as she recognises his for her: "Reader, I forgave him at the moment and on the spot. There was such deep remorse in his eye ... such unchanged love in his whole look and mien ..." (p.326). The direct address to the reader, as before, encourages sympathy for the character and fuller involvement in her difficulty.

She cannot bring herself to speak her forgiveness and the tension between her and Mr Rochester is conveyed as in many other exchanges between them; he is longing for her understanding, even her accusations, rather than silence, but she is so overcome by her dilemma that she cannot give him the reassurance he needs. When she shies away from his attempts to hold her, he speaks for her: "Why, Jane? I will spare you the trouble of much talking; I will answer for you — because I have a wife already, you would reply — I guess rightly?" (p.327). His understanding of her reaction is further demonstrated as he realises, "... you have no desire to expostulate, to upbraid, to make a scene: you are thinking how *to act* — *talking* you consider is of no use" (p.327).

Mr Rochester's bitterness against his being trapped into marriage with his first wife suggests her presence has seemed to place a curse on Thornfield for him, recalling his reaction to the house when he talked of it as gloomy and oppressive in an earlier chapter; the language used to describe it is hellish: "... this accursed place ... ghastliness of living death ... narrow stone hell, with its one real fiend ... that demon's vicinage ..." (p.328). His concern for duty and humanity are also shown as he admits he could have housed Bertha in a far more unhealthy property but chose to keep her guarded at Thornfield.

The confusion of motives between Mr Rochester and Jane is made clear as the reader knows she feels she must leave him, but he refers to the two of them still staying together, even if away from

Thornfield: "I have a place to repair to ... *you* are to share my solitude" (p.329). Jane's tender calming of his frenzied distress is completely selfless, as she herself is in the grip of the conflict with what she feels she ought to do; her tears are only allowed to flow to help him to recover himself: "Soon I heard him earnestly entreating me to be composed. I said I could not while he was in such a passion" (p.330). She admits her response is forced from her in respect of duty: "'I *do* love you,' I said, 'more than ever: but I must not show or indulge the feeling; and this is the last time I must express it'" (p.331).

Rochester does not want to understand what Jane says about leaving him; he deliberately misinterprets her words: "I pass over the madness about parting from me. You mean you must become a part of me" (p.331). He also refuses to acknowledge the truth of Bertha's existence, insisting, "... you shall yet be my wife: I am not married. You shall be Mrs Rochester ..." (p.331). Jane's determination not to be compromised shows the strength of the new kind of heroine Charlotte Bronte is depicting in the novel: equal to men in her control of her life, despite the distress it brings her: "If I lived with you as you desire — I should then be your mistress: to say otherwise is sophistical — is false" (p.331).

Rochester tells the story of his past: his marriage and the terrible life he has had, having been tricked into marriage without realising his wife was mad. The barrier of the untold past of Rochester is suggested as he speaks as if Jane were not there at first: "I forget she knows nothing of the character of that woman ..." (p.332). It is as if he is distanced from her by the weight of his experiences which she has not shared. When he brings himself to tell her the circumstances, it is a detailed, fluent account which clearly shows him as the victim, manipulated by others: "When I left college, I was sent to Jamaica, to espouse a bride already courted for me" (p.332). However, he does not spare himself blame: "Oh, I have no respect for myself when I think of that act!" (p.333). Again he shows how he was tricked, explaining for the reader as well as Jane the reason for his resentment, having learned too late of the madness in Bertha's family: "My father and my brother Rowland knew all this; but they thought only of the thirty thousand pounds, and joined in the plot against me" (p.333).

The desperation of Mr Rochester, and the frequent occasions when he looked tortured and troubled, are explained by the indication that he has suppressed his feelings and denied himself any emotional outlet for so long: "I restrained myself: I eschewed upbraiding, I curtailed remonstrance; I tried to devour my repentence and disgust in secret; I repressed the deep antipathy I felt" (p.333). The horrors of life with the mad, coarse and violent Bertha Mason are made even more disturbing for not being exactly detailed; Rochester makes a general summary of the dreadful situation, referring to "all the hideous and degrading agonies which must attend a man bound to a wife at once intemperate and unchaste" (p.334). This is realistic writing, as Rochester would want to spare Jane knowledge of actual activities and behaviour, but it also makes the tale all the more horrific through such hints and suggestions; the reader is left to his own imaginings about "a nature the most gross, impure, depraved I ever saw ..." (p.334).

Rochester's capacity for love and his need for comfort is shown when despite his pride, he is ready to accept Jane's pity. By using terms of natural family bonds, the author shows how desperately he longs for a normal relationship: "Your pity, my darling, is the suffering mother of love: its anguish is the very natal pang of divine passion. I accept it, Jane; let the daughter have free advent ..." (p.334). As he continues his story, the oppressive West Indian night Rochester describes reflects the emotional pressure he was suffering through his mad wife's foulness; the ugly imagery of the air "like sulphur-streams", the moon "broad and red, like a hot cannon-ball" (p.335), creates a vivid impression of an alien setting in which he was haunted by her "wolfish cries" (p.335).

The drama of this recounting of past suffering is brought to a climax with the reference to the idea of suicide, and the resolution and strength of Rochester is emphasised as he rejected this: "... it was true Wisdom that consoled me in that hour, and showed me the right path to follow" (p.335). The use of weather once again to reflect the feelings of characters is skilfully involved in Rochester's account, as the new spirit of hope in him is linked with "a wind fresh from Europe", which dispels the violent storm and replaces the oppressive atmosphere as "the air grew pure" (p.335).

The personification of Hope further dramatises the story Rochester tells, as he puts his thoughts and hopes for coping with the dreadful burden of his mad wife into a careful plan, as if he has outside aid: "'Go,' said Hope, 'and live again in Europe ...' I acted precisely on this suggestion" (p.336). More suggestive comments hint at the terrible experience of the journey to England: "... a fearful voyage I had with such a monster in the vessel" (p.336). The dreadful behaviour of Bertha since she was established in the third storey room at Thornfield is given a supernatural quality, linking with Jane's experience of her as a ghostly figure the night before her intended wedding, as her room is described as "a goblin's cell" (p.306).

Mr Rochester continues his story and tells of his reaction to meeting Jane when he returned to Thornfield. Despite his pleas, Jane feels she must not stay with him. During the description of the arrangements for Grace Poole's guardianship of Bertha, Jane is still quietly listening; she only occasionally prompts Rochester to continue; he comments on her capacity for encouraging his confidences; the implication is that he is enormously relieved to be able to unburden the whole tale to a sympathetic listener. "'Well, sir?' It is a small phrase very frequent with you; and which many a time has drawn me on and on through interminable talk ..." (p.337). He is encouraged to admit all the details even of his flitting from mistress to mistress, as if by recounting the whole story, he will somehow be able to put it behind him and find peace. His life before he met Jane once he returned to Europe is described as a continuous search for happiness, continually denied: "I longed only for what suited me — for the antipodes of the Creole: and I longed vainly" (p.338). The use of the geographical term, "antipodes", to suggest a complete opposite, further emphasises the idea of a continuous journey.

When Rochester's account finally comes to his meeting with Jane, she is described in supernatural terms, as if she is the good spirit in his life in contrast to Bertha as the evil spirit. Rochester refers to her as "my genius ... this elf" (p.339), and to a sense of being guided apart from his own will: "I must be aided, and by that hand: and aided I was" (p.339). The reader now sees the other side of the story of Jane's presence at Thornfield, and learns, as Jane does, of Rochester's intense interest in her: "... probably you were not aware that I thought of you ... I observed you ... I was vexed with you for getting out of my sight ... I liked what I had seen, and wished to see more" (pp.340-341). This method of narration continues to involve the reader in the same position as the character; at this stage of the novel, it is difficult to remember that Jane is supposedly telling the whole story and recalling Rochester's words to her.

The restraint Rochester had forced on himself is described in terms of tenderness towards a lovely tender plant; he was unwilling to harm Jane, yet desperate to love her: "I was for a while troubled with a haunting fear that if I handled the flower freely its bloom would fade ... such bloom and light and bliss rose to your young, wistful features, I had much ado often to avoid straining you then and there to my heart" (p.341). Jane's reactions are at last indicated and once again these are expressed in terms of the battle between desire and duty, "... his language was torture to me; for I knew what I must do — and do soon ... him who thus loved me I absolutely worshipped: and I must renounce love and idol" (p.342). This culminates in the response forced from her, the plain direct language suggesting she dare not say more or she would change her mind: "Mr Rochester, I will *not* be yours" (p.342).

Rochester tries to persuade her by emotional blackmail, as he knows she sympathises with him: "Give one glance to my horrible life when you are gone ... What shall I do, Jane? ... you condemn me to live wretched, and to die accursed?" (p.343). Jane's strength and resolution are extraordinary; she is determined not to shame either herself or him by an improper relationship; she is hardened by her previous experiences of hardship and strengthened by a moral code enforced on her when young: "Mr Rochester, I no more assign this fate to you than I grasp at it for myself. We were born to strive and endure — you as well as I: do so" (p.343). Rochester attempts to challenge this moral code; the author is exploring a fundamental question of philosophy in the dialogue: "Is it better to drive a fellow-creature to despair than to transgress a mere human law, no man being injured by the breech?" (p.343). Despite her desperate longing to accept Rochester's persuasions, Jane's sense of self worth, her independence which the author has been concerned to present throughout, asserts itself once again: "*I* care for myself. The more solitary, the more friendless, the more unsustained I am, the more I will respect myself" (p.344).

Jane is in terrible turmoil over her longing to remain at Thornfield and her strong moral obligations to an unlawful relationship; eventually she forces herself to leave in the early morning. Although in despair, Rochester admires this quality in Jane, "never was anything at once so frail and so indomitable" (p.344). Again he tries to appeal to her sensitivity and again she resists; the struggle is constantly reiterated; the leave taking is deliberately extended to show the torment both characters suffer: "What unutterable pathos was in his voice! How hard it was to reiterate firmly, 'I am going'" (p.345). Eventually once Jane has left Rochester and tries to sleep that night, the supernatural element of the novel is further developed in the vision of her mother which Jane experiences, again emphasising the strong moral code which has forced Jane to reject the possibility of happiness with Rochester, "... not a moon, but a white human form shone in the azure ... 'My daughter, flee temptation'" (p.346).

Jane's preparations and departure are described in detail to suggest that every move of collecting her possessions and passing the doors of those she has grown to love is difficult; yet again the struggle with her conscience is dramatised as she is tempted to enter Rochester's room; it is almost as if she is linked with the ghostly presence of her mother as she glides along and it is this which gives her the strength to resist: "My hand moved towards the lock: I caught it back, and glided on" (p.347).

The reference to the road ahead of Jane as she leaves Thornfield suggests the idea of her life as a journey, as previously indicated, and this is another stage, one of which she is frightened and uncertain as it is like "an awful blank" (p.347). The dread and insecurity she feels is powerfully suggested by linking her lack of awareness of her surroundings with a similar response of a condemned man walking to the gallows. The pain and despair Jane feels is poignantly conveyed; despite her resolution and determination, she suffers dreadfully at the thought of the pain she is also causing Rochester and the birds' singing seems a bitter mockery, "... birds were emblems of love. What was I? In the midst of my pain of heart and frantic effort of principle, I abhorred myself" (p.348). When finally in the coach on the way to a far-off place where she hopes Rochester will be unable to find her, Jane at last gives in to her feelings; the direct appeal is once again used to involve the reader in the distressing conflict of emotions: "... never may you, like me, dread to be the instrument of evil to what you wholly love" (p.348).

Questions on Chapter Twenty-seven

1. How does the author show the struggle Jane has in herself between duty and desire in this chapter?
2. How is the story of Rochester's marriage to Bertha Mason made dramatic?
3. What aspects of the characters of Jane, Rochester and Bertha Mason are emphasised in this chapter?

Glossary

P.326 Remorse: regret
P.326 Mien: attitude, appearance
P.327 Expostulate: argue, reason
P.327 Upbraid: reproach
P.328 Vicinage: area
P.329 Repair: withdraw, retreat
P.333 Eschewed: denied, rejected
P.333 Remonstrance: protest
P.333 Antipathy: dislike, hostility
P.334 Depraved: morally corrupt
P.338 Antipodes: direct opposite
P.345 Pathos: sadness
P.345 Reiterate: repeat

Chapter Twenty-eight

Summary

Jane gets out of the coach at Whitcross crossroads, and as it is evening, spends the night out of doors, sleeping in the shelter of a rock on the moors. The following day she has a humiliating struggle to find food and shelter, constantly being turned away from houses in the village. Eventually, led by a light she sees burning in a house across the moors, she staggers on until she is finally rescued and taken in by St John and his sisters.

Glossary

Jane turns to nature to protect her as she has lost all human contact and left her possessions on the coach. The chapter opens in the present tense, to add a sense of immediacy to the account of Jane's desolation; even the few possessions she took from Thornfield have been left in the coach; she has absolutely nothing and must depend on nature as a protector. The landscape is described as isolated, but not necessarily unfriendly; the moorland seems to offer a protective shelter: "There are great moors behind and on each hand of me; there are waves of mountains far beyond that deep valley at my feet ... I have no relative but the universal mother, Nature, I will seek her breast and ask repose" (p.349). The personification of nature suggests Jane's resourcefulness; having no human aid, she makes herself look at her surroundings in the most positive way she can: "Nature seemed to me benign and good ..." (p.350), and she eats bilberries and makes a bed tucked down by a large rock in the heathland. It is as if she has put off her human identity when she left Thornfield; she is exposed and vulnerable and must trust to natural support.

Jane's heart is personified also; this makes her sorrow seem even more intense: "It trembled for Mr Rochester ... it bemoaned ... it demanded ..." (p.350), and the image of the little bird with broken wings makes a pitiful impression of pain and distress: "... it still quivered its shattered pinions in vain attempts to seek him" (p.350). Jane's religious faith strengthens her and restores her spirit; convinced of the safety of herself and Mr Rochester because she has acted rightly, the sense of security in the wonder of the universe is effectively created in her response to the splendour of the Milky Way: "... what countless systems there swept space like a soft trace of light — I felt the might and strength of God" (p.351). The soft, gentle sounds in the description add to the sense of peace and comfort created.

Despite wishing she might have slipped away in death, when Jane wakes the following morning, her determination and strength of character are once more emphasised, "The burden must be carried; the want provided for; the suffering endured; the responsibility fulfilled. I set out" (p.351). The balanced phrases and the final short, direct statement show her staunch courage. The church bell Jane hears represents the world of human life, rather than that of the animals and insects she shared during the night. This sound gives her further reason to continue her journey but her pride stops her from asking for food. The detailed description of the inquiries she makes about work in the village she comes to shows her desperation; the short sentences suggest her lack of energy and shortness of breath due to hunger: "I must do something. What? I must apply somewhere. Where?" (p.352).

Jane suffers terrible hunger and tiredness as she fails to find work, shelter or food. The attractiveness of the cottage Jane approaches creates a more positive mood, "a pretty little house ... neat ... glittering ... mild-looking, cleanly-attired young woman", but this is dispelled when no encouragement is forthcoming, "... the white door closed, quite gently and civilly: but it shut me out" (p.353). Jane's desperate plight is powerfully conveyed by the details of her wanderings; even the parsonage offers no help as the clergyman is away. The repeated negatives in response to Jane's questions: "No ... No, he was gone ... Nay ..." (p.354), add to the sense of rejection which intensifies Jane's isolation. The attempt to barter for food further shows how desperate Jane has become and eventually her shame is overcome when she asks the farmer for bread, but she still retains some pride as she waits until "out of sight of his house" (p.355), before eating it. The final shreds of pride leave her when she asks for the porridge which might have been given to the pig; this part of the chapter vividly illustrates the degradation Jane is reduced to when she has forced herself away from the comforts of Thornfield.

Jane's journey over the moorland is described in powerful detail; it is an almost hallucinatory progress, as if it is all part of a dreadful nightmare: "My glazed eye wandered ... My eye still roved ... I sank down where I stood ... I dragged my exhausted limbs slowly ..." (p.356-357). The light Jane sees is described as a vision, a tantalising image continually drawing her forward, "... as it did not diminish, so it did not enlarge ... shining dim but constant through the rain ... now beamed from a sort of knoll ..." (p.357).

When Jane finally reaches the house in which the light is burning, it is described as attractive, clean and welcoming, with the "redness and radiance of a glowing peat fire" (p.358). The description of the young women working at their German with the old servant in the warmth and comfort of the kitchen creates a powerful contrast with Jane, tired, hungry and cold, outside looking in. The intriguing suggestion of a connection between Jane and the young ladies is hinted at in her reaction to seeing their faces: "I had nowhere seen such faces as theirs: and yet, as I gazed on them, I seemed intimate with every lineament" (p.358). The reader is introduced to these new characters in the novel in an unusual way; from snatches of overheard conversation, it becomes clear that they are in mourning for their father; that their brother is expected home; that they hope to become teachers when they have enlarged their own knowledge of foreign languages. The dialect of the servant woman, Hannah, is rough but friendly and the whole picture of the lifestyle of the household seems pleasant and comfortable. The reader is once again fully involved with Jane's experiences, finding out these details from her point of view and finally brought back to her circumstances, having with her "half-forgotten my own wretched position" (p.360).

Despite initial rejection, Jane is finally taken in by St John and his sisters. The suspicion of Hannah when Jane asks for food and shelter is realistically illustrated through the dialogue: "You should not be roving about now; it looks very ill ... I'm afeared you have some ill plans agate" (p.361). Finally the dramatic collapse of Jane, into "suffering ... anguish ... horror ... banishment" (p.361), is countered by rescue, which is introduced by an eerie echo of her despairing words: "'I can but die', I said ... 'All men must die ... but all are not condemned to meet a lingering and premature doom ...'" (pp.361-362). The voice coming out of the darkness is almost uncanny and this effect is extended in Jane's reaction: "terrified at the unexpected sound ..." (p.362).

The speaker explains to Hannah: "You have done your duty in excluding, now let me do mine in admitting her" (p.362); this concern for duty in the speaker's attitude is to be expanded later. The desperate state of Jane's travel weariness and hunger is effectively suggested by the sense of wonder that she is now in the "clean, bright kitchen — on the very hearth" — where she had longed to be, and "trembling, sickening ... wild, and weather-beaten" (p.362).

The sense of loss of identity previously suggested by the isolation of Jane on the moorland is added to when she is described as "worn to nothing" (p.362), and increased further when she adopts the alias of Jane Elliott, but under the influence of the tender care of the sisters, she "began once more to know myself" (p.363). Her earliest sense of trust in Nature to guard her is applied to the human world, trusting in the good nature she has sensed in her rescuers: "If I were a masterless and stray dog, I know that you would not turn me from your hearth tonight: as it is, I have no fear" (p.363). The comfort and restoration of a sense of security she finds are movingly suggested in an image of light at the end of the chapter, where her constant faith is shown once more: "I thanked God — experienced amidst unutterable exhaustion a glow of grateful joy — and slept" (p.364).

Questions on Chapter Twenty-eight

1. How is Jane's determination and strength shown in this chapter?
2. Show how the author makes Jane's distress and hunger realistic.
3. How is the reader kept involved in Jane's journey and her eventual rescue?

Glossary

P.361 Agate: intended
P.362 Premature: earlier than normal, advanced

Chapter Twenty-nine

Summary

Jane stays in bed for three days and nights, unable to move or respond to her rescuers, though she is aware of their conversations about her. When she is strong enough, she comes down to the kitchen and is given background information on the family by Hannah. She is concerned to find herself work and not to be dependent on the Rivers family any longer than she can help. She refuses to talk about Thornfield or Rochester and his household, insisting that she has no home or friends or family.

Commentary

Jane's condition and situation is discussed by St John Rivers and his sisters. Jane's exhaustion is well described as she recalls being unaware of time for three days and nights after being taken in by St John. The physical fatigue is described as a kind of paralysis: "I lay on it motionless as a stone ... to open my lips or move my limbs was equally impossible" (p.365). Her sensitivity and concern over being thought a burden is a link with her childhood when she was constantly considered a nuisance; the author shows how this attitude once formed, is part of her for life. She has a feeling Hannah "wished me away" (p.365), but is comforted when she does not in the sisters' conversations "hear a syllable of regret at the hospitality they had extended to me" (p.365).

The emphasis on Jane's plain looks when St John is discussing her with his sisters enforces the idea of a different kind of heroine in this novel; Jane is an independent woman; she does not submit or succumb to the dominance of male figures in the story and she does not fit into the traditional pattern of a romantic heroine, beautiful and passive. Both these aspects are suggested in St John's comments: "I trace lines of force in her face which make me sceptical of her tractability ... She looks sensible, but not at all handsome" (p.366).

The idea that Jane has come through a trial, a testing period, during her terrible journey across the moors, is implied in the description of her clothing having been cleansed, not just cleaned but cleared of associations of her past life and the stress of her moral dilemma over leaving Rochester. Her shoes and stockings are described as "purified"; in her outfit there is "no speck of dirt, no trace of the disorder I so hated, and which seemed so to degrade me ..." (p.366). This could also suggest that she does not want to acknowledge the more dangerous, disturbing side of her nature; her desires, represented by the dirt which distresses her, are repressed by her dedication to duty represented by her "clean and respectable-looking" appearance.

Jane recovers enough to come down to the kitchen and talk to Hannah, who is clearly devoted to the young people and proudly tells Jane about their lives and accomplishments. The blunt speech of Hannah and her reproving attitude towards the idea of Jane begging is a reminder of Bessie and her warmth, hidden under a brusque attitude. Hannah "bustled about" (p.367), as Bessie did, and has the same respect for education, also a similar lack of imagination towards someone who acts in an unexpected manner: "Are you book-learned? ... Whatever cannot ye keep yourself for, then?" (p.367). Jane's restraint and control, developed significantly in contrast to her outbursts as a child, are shown in her response to Hannah's question about her begging: "I was indignant for a moment, but remembering that anger was out of the question ... I answered quietly" (p.367). The moral outlook of the author, setting human sympathy higher than material values, is made plain later in the conversation with Hannah when Jane has confirmed details of the family at Moor House: "... you just now made it a species of reproach that I had no 'brass' and no house. Some of the best people that ever lived have been as destitute as I am; and if you are a Christian, you ought not to consider poverty a crime" (p.369).

The use of Hannah as narrator in this section of the chapter is a skilful way of filling in details of the family's background for the reader in a realistic manner; her respect and admiration for the young people again recalls Bessie's support and regard for Jane in contrast with the Reed children: "There was nothing like them in these parts, nor ever had been" (p.369). The concern for propriety in the Rivers household is clear in the response of the sisters to finding Jane in the kitchen with Hannah, "Mary and I sit in the kitchen sometimes, because at home we like to be free, even to licence — but you are a visitor, and must go into the parlour" (p.370). The tidiness and formality of the parlour, "There was no superfluous ornament in the room" (p.371), further emphasises the concern for respectability and rigid control which is also reflected in St John, sitting so stiff and still that "Had he been a statue instead of a man, he could not hve been easier" (p.371). His attitude to Jane's renewed appetite again shows concern for order and control: "Now you may eat, though still not immoderately" (p.372). There is a lack of humanity implied in his manner; although he is kind to have taken Jane in at all, it is very clearly seen as an act of duty and there is no hint of emotional spontaneity in his nature.

Jane refuses to explain her recent past and her obstinacy reveals a similar resolution in St John with regard to his duty. Jane's determination and resolve are shown as she resists the Rivers' attempts to find out about her background; when St John suggests writing to inform some friends of her whereabouts, her reaction is definite and unyielding: "That, I must plainly tell you, is out of my power to do; being absolutely without home and friends" (p.372). The hardness previously indicated in St John's rigidity and control is shown again as he does not tactfully look away when Jane is embarrassed by the reference to marriage, as his sisters do: "... the colder and sterner brother continued to gaze, till the trouble he had excited forced out tears as well as colour" (p.372).

This determination and rigidity on each side builds up tension between Jane and St John, suggested by Jane's reference to him as her "penetrating young judge" (p.373). She recognises his generosity and righteousness, however, despite the lack of emotional sympathy, in her acknowledgement: "... you have rescued me, by your noble hospitality, from death. This benefit conferred gives you an unlimited claim on my gratitude ..." (p.373). When she has recounted as much of her former and recent past as she feels she can, Jane makes it clear that she recognises the very different attitudes of St John and his sisters, the one dutiful and the others more naturally kindly, "I owe to their spontaneous, genuine, genial compassion as large a debt as to your evangelical charity" (p.374). St John recognises Jane's perception in making this distinction between them, and his image of the frozen bird, which his sisters would take pleasure in keeping whereas he would prefer to help Jane to keep herself, further enforces the contrast. Jane's admirable determination to do whatever work she must, to begin to once more make her own way in the world, ends the chapter in a positive and encouraging atmosphere; the reader is encouraged to follow on with the character to see how she will cope with another stage in her life.

Questions on Chapter Twenty-nine

1. What is the importance of Hannah in this chapter?
2. What impression of St John Rivers is given in this chapter?
3. How do Jane's reactions to her treatment at Moor House reflect her personality and attitudes?

Glossary

P.369 Destitute: totally poor, without any means of support
P.374 Genial: friendly, pleasant

Chapter Thirty

Summary

Jane settles in with the Rivers family for a short while until the sisters go to positions as governesses and St John resumes his duties as clergyman. St John finds Jane a position as schoolmistress for the village school for girls which he has just opened. The Rivers receive news of their uncle John's death.

Commentary

Jane enjoys the company and instruction of the Rivers sisters. Jane's happiness in the company of the Rivers sisters is shown in the delight she takes in their home and surroundings and the pleasure she finds in the similarity of their tastes. The harmonious atmosphere is shown through the repetition of positive verbs, "... enjoyed ... delighted ... approved ... loved ..." (p.376), and the sense of Jane being both spiritually and physically restored by the surroundings is suggested in the image of nourishment "... my eye feasted on the outline of swell and sweep ... so many pure and sweet sources of pleasure" (p.376). The novelty for Jane of being taught rather than teaching is shown to be another source of pleasure and the mutual delight in each other's company is shown in the balanced phrases of the description of Diana teaching Jane German: "I saw the part of instructress pleased and suited her; that of scholar pleased and suited me no less" (p.377).

The hardness and rigidity of St John noted in the previous chapter is extended in the suggestion that a barrier is set up around him: "he seemed of a reserved, an abstracted, and even of a brooding nature" (pp.377-378). There is a suggestion of repression of passion in him, as when Jane sees him deep in thought, she notices "the frequent flash and changeful dilation of his eye" (p.378). He seems to deliberately deny taking pleasure in his surroundings, or responding to nature, as if this would be self indulgent: "never did he seem to roam the moors for the sake of their soothing silence" (p.378), thus his energies and emotions have no outlet and are unnaturally restrained. This impression is reinforced by the description of the sermon he delivers, the force which is "compressed, condensed, controlled" and seems to Jane to be prompted by "troubling impulses of insatiate yearnings and disquieting aspirations" (p.378).

When the family prepares to depart from Moor House, Jane asks about work for herself and after long hesitation, St John eventually suggests the post of village schoolmistress. A reminder of the treatment of Jane by the Ingrams is given when she describes the circumstances in which the Rivers sisters will be governesses: "in families by whose wealthy and haughty members they were regarded only as humble dependents ..." (p.379); this is in contrast to Jane's admiration of their skills and appreciation of their sensitivity, showing again the author's concern for human sympathy and the value of the individual. Jane's anxiety for work for herself once she knows the Rivers sisters are soon to move and the house is to be shut up, is shown in her insistence in questioning St John as to any situation he may have found for her; his hesitancy in telling her is skilfully used to draw out the suspense and keep the reader guessing, like the character. St John hints and suggests but at first says nothing definite: "I have nothing eligible or profitable to suggest ... since I am myself poor and obscure, I can offer you but a service of poverty and obscurity ... how poor the proposal is — how trivial ..." (pp. 380-381). When eventually the position of teacher at the newly opened school for the girls of the village is suggested, it seems very appealing after all the hints of a menial situation. For Jane, typically, one of the main attractions is that she will be independent, and it appeals to her sense of decorum as "it was not ignoble — not unworthy — not mentally degrading" (p.381).

St John's repressed passion is again suggested in his reaction to Jane's acceptance of the post, thinking she will become restless, as he recognises in her the passionate nature he denies in himself: "human affections and sympathies have a most powerful hold on you" (p.382). He further acknowledges this side of his own nature: "I ... almost rave in my restlessness" (p.382). His sister also confirms it: "He will sacrifice all to his long-framed resolves ... natural affection and feelings more potent still" (p.383). Through the characters, Jane in her denial of her love for Rochester and St John in his denial of his passions, the author is questioning this repression in the name of duty, seeing it as morally right but possibly not appropriate to full humanity.

The reference to the letter announcing the Rivers' uncle's death is one of the skilful interconnections between characters introduced by the author, but it is not followed up in this chapter. The earlier occurence of a letter from an Uncle John to Mrs Reed which had prompted Jane to write in the hopes of gaining some financial independence had not been resolved either, thus the comment about the "one other person, not more closely related than we ... he has bequeathed every penny to the other relation ..." hints at, but does not explore, the connection. The author is thus involving the reader in the gradually unfolding mystery and irony of the situation in which Jane is to be the beneficiary of money gained by a relative who had been responsible for ruining the Rivers' father.

Questions on Chapter Thirty

1. How is the friendly and encouraging atmosphere of the Rivers' home shown in this chapter?
2. How does the author make the contrast between St John and his sisters clear?

3. What general concerns of the author's are explored through the events in this chapter?
4. What means does the author use to keep the reader involved in this stage of Jane's story?

Glossary

P.378 Abstracted: removed, distanced
P.378 Dilation: enlarging, widening
P.378 Insatiate: unsatisfied
P.378 Disquieting: disturbing, troublesome
P.378 Aspirations: desires, ambitions
P.381 Eligible: worthy

Chapter Thirty-one

Summary

Jane is installed as the village schoolmistress. St John Rivers calls on her to see how she is settling in and brings a present of painting materials from his sisters. While he is talking of his decision to become a missionary, Miss Oliver, the hieress who has funded the school, comes to visit and tries to persuade St John to accompany her home and visit her father. He refuses as he has forced himself to deny the relationship with Rosamond in order to follow his duty to go abroad.

Commentary

Jane tries to make the best of her situation but cannot help thinking about the contrasting life she might have had as Mr Rochester's wife. The opening of the chapter stresses Jane's insecurity and longing for a place to call her own, as the humble school cottage is welcomed because "I at last find a home" (p.385). The present tense is used to involve the reader directly in the immediacy of the character's situation: "I am sitting alone on the hearth" (p.385). The honesty of the character is shown as she admits some resentment at her lowly position and the difficulty of teaching the ignorant village children: "I felt — yes, idiot that I am — I felt degraded" (p.385). This is also shown in the sense of forcing herself to accept her new circumstances: "I must not forget ... My duty will be ... I shall strive ..." (p.385).

The temptation of the desire to be with Mr Rochester and live in luxury is effectively described as a "silken snare" (p.386), apparently lovely yet dangerous; again Jane is involved in a conflict between her desires and her devotion to duty, what she wants and what she feels she ought to do. She further refers to her picture of the life she has denied herself as "... a fool's paradise ... delusive bliss" (p.386), and turns her thoughts to Mr Rochester himself, as so often thinking of others rather than herself.

St John's conversation further reveals a similarity between himself and Jane in, as Jane has already noted, his determination to do his duty and reject his desires. St John's appearance interrupts her thoughts and the present he brings shows the difference between himself and his sisters. They have given her something practical in the painting materials, which she can occupy herself with and take her mind off her difficult situation; he has merely moral instruction to offer: "I counsel you to resist firmly every temptation which would incline you to look back ..." (p.387). He seems to be deliberately emphasising the less attractive aspects of her new situation, suggesting she may have found the "work harder ... perhaps your accomodations ... have disappointed ... you feel solitude an oppression?" (p.387) but this shows his perception and his understanding of someone like himself who has strong passions and has had to deny them.

Jane is clearly unwilling to admit to negative feelings; her pride will not let her, for although she has admitted to herself the "lonely vale of Morton" (p.386), she insists to St John that "I have hardly had time yet to enjoy a sense of tranquillity, much less to grow impatient under one of loneliness" (p.387). Another indication that St John realises Jane has a spirit much like his own is that he admits his own sense of frustration to her: "A year ago I was myself intensely miserable, because I thought I had made a mistake in entering the ministry ... I burned for the more active life of the world ..." (p.388). The extravagance of his language shows his rather elevated view of himself and his calling, perhaps a way of convincing himself that he is doing the right thing in deciding to become a missionary: "my powers heard a call from Heaven to rise, gather their full strength, spread their wings, and mount beyond ken" (p.388).

His determination is emphasised by the insistence in his tone and the imagery of struggle used: "... I resolved ... broken through ... cut asunder ... conflict ... I *will* overcome ..." (p.388). The appearance of Miss Oliver is deliberately introduced at this point in the chapter to show one of the 'entanglements' from which St John had to break free, as did Jane, denying his desire for the sake of duty. The contrast of his stern voice and resolute manner with the light, lively tone and manner of Rosamond is made clear by the description of her voice: "sweet as a silver bell ... those musical accents" (pp.388-389).

Rosamond Oliver creates a contrast of mood with her lively manner, beautiful appearance and talk of socialising. The description of Rosamond Oliver has a supernatural quality; she seems the complete image of a traditional romantic heroine, pure, beautiful and virtuous, "A vision ... a form clad in pure white ... a face of perfect beauty ... no defect was perceptible ... sweetly formed ..." (p.389). Jane sums her up as "this earthly angel" (p.389), and the author clearly implies the difference between her attractiveness and Jane's plain appearance, emphasising her choice of a different kind of heroine for her central character, with personality more important than looks.

The reader is reminded of the superior attitude of the Ingrams towards Jane when Miss Oliver remarks on coming to see Jane; she is referred to almost as an object: "'... this is she?' pointing to me. 'It is,' said St John" (p.389). This is not meant unkindly; it is quite innocent in Miss Oliver as she would naturally treat a village schoolmistress as her social inferior, especially as she provided the funds for her salary and arranged for her accomodation and assistant. It is clear that this is another aspect of humiliation for Jane; however, she shows her tolerance and understanding as she recognises Miss Oliver's "direct and naive simplicity of tone and manner" (p.390), as she asks if all is satisfactory for Jane.

Miss Oliver represents the world which Jane and St John rejected as not rightfully theirs; she talks of "dancing till two o'clock" (p.390), and tempts St John with invitations to her home to see her father: "You are quite a stranger ... will you return with me ... Do come and see papa" (p.391). Her insistence is shown in the repetition and Jane's understanding is shown as she notices what a difficult struggle St John has with himself when he makes himself refuse her; though she says he was the only one to know, clearly she recognises the difficulty he is in: "Mr St John spoke almost like an automaton: himself only knew the effort it cost him thus to refuse" (p.391).

Questions on Chapter Thirty-one

1. What details are given in this chapter of the lifestyle of Jane in Morton?
2. How are similarities shown in the characters and attitudes of Jane and St John Rivers?
3. What is the author's purpose in introducing Miss Oliver in this chapter?

Glossary

P.386 Snare: trap
P.386 Delusive: pretend, unreal
P.387 Tranquility: calm, peacefulness
P.391 Automaton: robot, mechanical creature

Chapter Thirty-two

Summary

Jane gradually comes to enjoy her work more and finds pleasure in the company of some of the families of her pupils. She is invited to the Olivers' home after Rosamond has discovered she can draw and sits for a picture. St John confides more of his feelings about Rosamond to Jane but continues in his determination to give her up and become a missionary.

Commentary

Jane has an outwardly calm existence but is troubled by disturbing dreams. This makes her particularly sensitive to St John's similar situation. Jane's developing contentment in her work is shown in this chapter by the detailed description of her variety of pupils in the opening paragraphs; the pleasure she finds in those who enjoy their work and try to improve themselves reflects her own efforts and continues the author's theme of the importance and value of education. The social life Jane gains through association with the families of her older pupils shows how she is becoming part of the community: "I passed many a pleasant evening hour in their own homes" (p.392).

This satisfaction and contentment is shown to be rather superficial, however, as Jane's subconscious self and her real desires are shown in the description of her dream. The calm of her outward life is contrasted by the wildness and excitement of her dream world: "... many-coloured, agitated, full of the ideal, the stirring, the stormy ... I still again and again met Mr Rochester, always at some exciting crisis ..." (p.393). As so often, the author effectively makes the reader involved with the feelings of her central character by describing the emotional response in physical terms: "I rose ... trembling and quivering ... the convulsion of despair ..." (p.393).

The temptation of St John continues with Rosamond Oliver's frequent visits to the school. Jane's disapproval is shown in her perceptive comment: "Of course, she knew her power" (p.393), and in the observation that "she generally came at the hour when Mr Rivers was engaged in giving his daily catechizing lesson" (p.393). The passion restrained in St John is made clear by the references to heat and light: "... his cheek would glow ... his eye burn ..." (p.393), and the admiration of his resolve is shown in Jane's remark that "he would not give one chance of heaven, nor relinquish, for the elysium of her love, one hope of the true, eternal Paradise" (p.394).

Rosamond is attracted to Jane and becomes friendly with her, sitting for a portrait and inviting her to Vale Hall. Jane sternly sums up the character of Rosamond, balancing her good qualities against those not so attractive; the language is balanced and careful just like her observations, but she admits: "I liked her almost as I liked my pupil Adele" (p.394). She shows a kind of superiority in this comment; clearly she looks on Miss Oliver as a child in comparison with herself, having had very little hardship or difficulty in her life, whereas Jane had to grow up very early and take responsibility for herself in a harsh world. Rosamond's excitement at finding Jane's pictures shows this childlike quality, emphasised in the frequent exclamations and questions, and the exaggeration of the description of her reaction: "She was first transfixed with surprise, and then electrified with delight" (p.395).

Jane's talent and pleasure in her work furthers her relationship with Miss Oliver and leads to the meeting with Mr Oliver, described in very effective terms in contrast with his daughter, who "looked like a bright flower near a hoary turret" (p.395). The romantic language shows Jane is at ease and happier, and once she is invited to visit the Olivers' home and is recognised as "clever enough to be a governess in a high family" (p.395), she feels far more content: "I thought I would far rather be where I am ..." (p.395).

Jane's respect for, and admiration of, St John is extended when she realises that there would be no objection to a marriage between him and Rosamond from her father, who "evidently regarded the young clergyman's good birth, old name, and sacred profession as sufficient compensation for the want of fortune" (p.396). Her noting of this fact shows her interest in, and concern for, him; his for her is shown as he comes to see her on the holiday and brings her poetry. The author's digression at this point is almost directly in her own voice, rather than her character's, and shows how concerned she was for the recognition of the value of literature, in an increasingly materialistic age: "I know poetry is not dead, nor genius lost; nor has Mammon gained power over either, to bind or slay ..." (p.396). The dramatic language and the personification of greed is the image of Mammon, the god of selfish love of riches, shows her strength of feeling.

Jane's offer of a copy of her picture of Rosamond to St John encourages him to confide more of his feelings and intentions to her. Jane's understanding and perception are shown again as she recognises St John's concern at the sight of the picture of Rosamond she has painted; she acknowledges her own tendency to suppress her feelings in the recognition of his: "he tasks himself too far: locks every feeling and pang within ..." (p.397). Jane's inner feelings are expressed in her wild dreams; she knows that they have to have some kind of release and thus realises: "I am sure it would benefit him to talk a little about this sweet Rosamond, whom he thinks he ought not to marry ... solitude is at least as bad for you as it is for me" (p.397). Her generosity in offering him a copy of her picture, "Would it comfort, or would it wound you to have a similar painting?" (p.398), shows her insight and he recognises this as he has previously responded to her sensitivity: "That I should like to have it is certain: whether it would be judicious or wise is another question" (p.398).

The extraordinary control St John exercises over his feelings is made almost absurd when he allows himself a little indulgence of listening to Jane telling him Rosamond likes him: "he actually took out his watch and laid it upon the table to measure the time" (p.398). Jane's ease and confidence with St John is clearly shown to have developed considerably since her first awkward conversations with him at Moor House, as she can even suggest that perhaps it would be better if he did marry Rosamond after all. The imagery used to illustrate his rejection of the temptation of a married life with Rosamond shows how thoroughly traditional religious ideas have affected him: "there is an asp in the garland: the wine has a bitter taste: her promises are hollow — her offers false: I see and know all this" (p.399).

Although Jane has similar high moral standards, the language suggests that she finds his reaction extreme, that the rigidity with which he holds these beliefs may spoil his life and unnaturally repress his energies. He is forcing himself to deny the reality of his desire for the sake of an unrealistic, exalted vision of his duty: "My foundation laid on earth for a mansion in heaven? My hopes of being numbered in the band who have merged all ambitions in the glorious one of bettering their race ..." (p.400). Jane knows how deeply the dilemma is affecting him: "You speak coolly enough; but you suffer in the conflict. You are wasting away" (p.400). Her boldness is similar to that she showed when challenging Mr Rochester about his feelings; her spirited nature and self-respect are shown once again: "He had not imagined that a woman would dare to speak so to a man. For me, I felt at home in this sort of discourse" (p.400).

The misinterpretation of the creed St John says he follows is suggested in the contradiction of his comments, as he insists he is "a cold, hard, ambitious man ... Reason, and not feeling, is my guide", yet says he adopts Christ's "pure, His merciful, His benignant doctrines ..." (p.401). This implies that he does not, in fact, allow himself mercy or kindness, and relentlessly drives himself on in the belief that this is the only way he can usefully serve his religion "Of the ambition to win power and renown for my wretched self she has formed the ambition to spread my Master's Kingdom, to achieve victories for the standard of the Cross" (p.401). The language is elaborate and splendid, like traditional hymns, but does not have the sincerity of simplicity, suggesting it is forced and the ideas and motivation are imposed.

The final paragraphs of the chapter introduce another trace of mystery, as St John tears off a small strip from the paper Jane uses to cover her drawing to prevent it getting dirty; he has clearly made some connection with Jane's appearance as he seemed to "make a note of every point in my shape, face, and dress" (p.401); the author cleverly diverts yet increases the reader's curiosity by implying that they should take the same course as Jane: "I dismissed, and soon forgot it" (p.402).

Questions on Chapter Thirty-two

1. How is the relationship between Jane and St John developed in this chapter?
2. What does the reader learn about St John's feelings about Rosamond and his struggle to deny these?
3. How is Jane shown to be settling in to the community of Morton?

Glossary

P.393 Catechizing: religiously instructing
P.394 Relinquish: give up
P.394 Elysium: heaven
P.398 Judicious: sensible

P.399 Asp: deadly poisonous snake
P.401 Benignant: kind

Chapter Thirty-three

Summary

St John visits Jane despite a snowstorm and eventually tells her of her uncle's death and the legacy he has left her. This is the fortune which the Rivers family did not get because of a quarrel. Jane learns from St John that he and his sisters are in fact her cousins, and is delighted and determined to share the money equally between the four of them.

Commentary

St John's appearance disturbs Jane and a sense of anticipation is built up. The description of the snowstorm at the beginning of the chapter prepares the reader for some upheaval; as so often in the novel, the weather has foreshadowed events in the characters' lives. Jane's agitation and concern at the appearance of St John also adds to this sense of unease, as does the dramatic description of his arrival, as he "came in out of the frozen hurricane, the howling darkness ... the cloak that covered his tall figure all white as a glacier" (p.403). The uncertainty continues when he has only come "to have a little talk with you", yet "I have had hard work to get here, I assure you" (p.403).

The hard coldness of temperament which St John has developed to repress his passionate nature is emphasised, not only in the description of him looking like a glacier, but also in Jane's consideration of him, "... very cool and collected ... like chiselled marble ... pale brow and cheek as pale ..." (p.404). This coldness is shown to be unnerving to Jane, and his lack of conversation, even though he said he came to talk, disturbs her even more, forcing her to speak to break the uncomfortable silence, "Thinking it urgent to say something ... nor could I, in my impatience, consent to be dumb ..." (p.404). The conversation between them is extremely stilted on his part, however; the short abrupt sentences, "Does he? ... I know ..." (p.405), add to the creation of tension in this section of the chapter before he at last starts on his story.

The story is gradually told and connections are made with earlier hints in the novel. When the story is clearly Jane's, the author's skill in linking coincidences is evident, as the revelation of St John knowing her past through Briggs' letter is made realistic by the restrained tone of St John's account, only calmly suggesting: "... there are parallel points in her history and yours ... again, your fates are analogous ..." (p.406). The drama is all on Jane's side and directed to her true feelings as she immediately demands news of Mr Rochester, her repeated questions showing her agitation and distress: "what of Mr Rochester? How and where is he? What is he doing? Is he well?" (p.406). The connection with St John's strange reaction to Jane's painting in the previous chapter is also explained, again in a restrained and therefore more believable way, when Jane recognises the "shabby slip of paper, hastily torn off ... in my own handwriting, the words 'JANE EYRE'" (p.407), which reveal her real name rather than her alias, Jane Elliott.

The news of Jane's inheritance is also given in the most calm and almost indifferent manner; clearly St John is shown to have restrained his feelings to an almost unnatural degree, as he and his sisters are the losers to Jane's gain: "Merely to tell you that your uncle, Mr Eyre of Madiera, is dead; that he has left you all his property, and that you are now rich — merely that — nothing more" (p.407). The repetition of "merely" suggests some hint of sarcasm in St John's tone, perhaps, but the lack of dramatic excitement makes the situation described easier to relate to. Jane is immediately concerned by the consequences of suddenly attaining wealth, rather than delighting in the situation; thus the author maintains her credibility as a character; the restraint she also imposed on herself is emphasised in this, through her direct address to the reader: "One does not jump, and spring, and shout hurrah! at hearing one has got a fortune; one begins to consider responsibilities ..." (p.408).

St John's hint of sarcasm is developed in his remark about leaving Jane "to your sorrows" (p.409), and this tone seems to alert Jane to the underlying irony of the situation, as she then asks about the connection between St John and Mr Briggs. The suspense of the story is maintained in St John's reluctance to explain: "the clergy are often appealed to about odd matters ... Another time ... I would rather not just now" (p.409). When the connection between them as relations is eventually made, the imagery is powerful and dramatic in contrast to the language of the earlier part of the chapter: "Circumstances knit themselves, fitted themselves, shot into order: the chain that had been lying hitherto a formless lump of links was drawn out straight" (p.410).

Jane is far more pleased about her relatives than the money, and determines to share it with them. Jane's delight in realising that she has some living relatives is also made clear through excited and lively language, thus emphasising by the contrast how much more people mean to her than material possessions, recalling her reactions to the jewels and rich clothes Mr Rochester attempted to press on her: "Glorious discovery to a lonely wretch! This was wealth indeed! ... I now clapped my hands in sudden joy — my pulse bounded, my veins thrilled" (p.411). Her immediate desire to share her good fortune confirms her generous and loving nature as frequently shown before: "Now the wealth did not weigh on me: now it was not a mere bequest of coin — it was a legacy of life, hope, enjoyment" (p.411).

It is the independence which the money brings which is so stimulating to Jane; she now has the power to achieve the home and family for which she has yearned for so long. Her language is determined and direct: "What I want is, that you should write to your sisters and tell them of the fortune that has accrued to them ... I will have a home and connexions. I like Moor House, and I will live at Moor House ..." (p.412). The repetition of "I want ... I will" confirms the new confidence that news of the legacy has given her. Her spirited nature asserts itself also, when St John tries to protest at her plans: "Brother? Yes; at the distance of a thousand leagues! Sisters? Yes; slaving amongst strangers! I wealthy — gorged with gold I never earned and do not merit!" (p.413). Again the dramatic quality of the language in contrast to earlier restraint adds to the sense of delight mixed with ridicule of his resistance; the frequent exclamation marks suggest an almost childlike excitement such as Jane was denied in her earlier years.

Questions on Chapter Thirty-three

1. How does the author build up suspense before the news of Jane's fortune is revealed?
2. How are contrasting aspects of Jane's character shown in this chapter?
3. Explain in your own words the connection between Jane and the Rivers family and how it came to be made clear.

Glossary

P.404 Chiselled: cut
P.406 Analogous: parallel, similar
P.413 Stuffed: overwhelmed

Chapter Thirty-four

Summary

Jane refurbishes Moor House to make it attractive and homely for the Rivers sisters to spend Christmas there and re-establish their life in Morton. St John frequently insists Jane should take on worthwhile work, starts to influence her studies and eventually asks her to come out to India with him as a missionary wife. Jane, after a struggle with her conscience and thoughts of Mr Rochester, comes to a decision to accept the idea if she can go as his sister, rather than his wife, but St John cannot accept this.

Commentary

Jane finishes her time as village schoolmistress and prepares Moor House for family life again. Jane's involvement and sense of self-worth in her teaching are shown clearly in the description of her reactions as she closes the school for Christmas, knowing that someone else will take her place as schoolmistress. Her pleasure in the "decent, respectable, modest and well-informed young women" (p.415), shows her own concern for high standards and her reference to "my Morton girls" shows her pride in them and happiness in her achievements. St John's stern manner and concern for devotion to duty is shown in the suggestion of his disapproval of Jane's readiness to leave the school apart from the hour's instruction she has promised the brighter girls: "Would not a life devoted to the task of regenerating your race be well spent?" (p.415).

Jane's more realistic viewpoint is shown as she intends to enjoy her new wealth in a positive way, by no means selfishly, as she hopes to restore the life and beauty of Moor House for her new-found cousins: "My purpose, in short, is to have all things in an absolutely perfect state of readiness for Diana and Mary before next Thursday" (p.416). The contrast between her natural pleasure and St John's unnatural denial is shown clearly in their conversation with his constant recommendations to behave dutifully: "... look beyond Moor House and Morton, and sisterly society and the selfish calm and sensual comfort of civilised affluence" (p.417), and her direct retort: "I feel I have adequate cause to be happy, and I will be happy". His words have a harsh, almost sinister quality with the repetitions of 's' and 'c' sounds, changing something delightful into something to be scorned; as before, illustrating the extremity of his code, going beyond natural Christian feeling.

The delight in homemaking Jane experiences is shown in the detailed description of the furnishings she buys and installs in the house, and the satisfied summary of her achievements further emphasises this: "as complete a model of bright modest snugness ..." (p.417). St John's denial of pleasure, for others as well as himself, is cruelly disappointing to Jane, as she eagerly shows him around the refurbished house, "but not a syllable did he utter, indicating pleasure in the improved aspect of his abode" (p.418). Jane's direct address, "I did not like this, reader" (p.418), shows her spirited attitude, and her further remarks on St John show, as so often, that her concern is for others rather than herself: "The humanities and amenities of life had no attraction for him — its peaceful enjoyments no charm" (p.418). Her understanding and sympathy are clear, though there may be a touch of ridicule at his extremity, in her realisation that "This parlour is not his sphere ... the Himalayan ridge, or Caffre bush, even the plague-cursed Guinea Coast swamp, would suit him better" (p.419). The contrast with St John's sisters recalls Jane's first comparisons, as they show most reassuring delight in their surroundings: "I had the pleasure of feeling that my arrangements met their wishes exactly, and that what I had done added a vivid charm to their joyous return home" (p.419).

St John continues to put his duty above his desires and denies himself any pleasure or comfort. He begins to constantly watch Jane as she studies with her cousins. The determination of St John not to allow himself pleasure and comfort is yet further emphasised when he agrees to go out to a dying woman despite the dreadful weather outside; again Jane's understanding of his compulsive self-denial is shown in her reaction on his return: "He had performed an act of duty; made an exertion; felt his own strength to do and deny, and was on better terms with himself" (p.420). His repression of emotion is also illustrated further in this chapter, when he gives the news of Rosamond Oliver's intended marriage to Mr Granby, instead of his sisters' wished-for union with him. He is described as "serene as glass" (p.421), the image suggesting the cold hardness he had described in himself, and the idea of reflecting the expressions of others rather than showing anything of himself. As before, he uses imagery of conflict to describe the situation, when he does eventually comment on it to Jane: "You see, Jane, the battle is fought and the victory won" (p.421).

There are gradual hints of St John's intentions towards Jane as the chapter develops, his frequent glances at the table where the three young women worked, "with a curious intensity of observation", his "satisfaction" at her conscientious visits to teach at the school, his comment that Jane is "better calculated to endure variations of climate than many more robust" (p.422). The sense of foreboding Jane has when he searchingly stares at her, "as if I was sitting in the room with something uncanny" (p.422), and the plan to have her learn Hindustani, apparently to "assist him" (p.423), connect with the other examples and prepare the reader for his later proposal and her rejection. She finds the experience only disturbing: "I fell under a freezing spell ... I wished, many a time, he had continued to neglect me" (p.423). The cold image suggests that there would be no tenderness, no emotional support offered in any relationship with him. This is further confirmed in similar imagery when he kisses her, only at the insistence of his sister: "There are no such things as marble kisses or ice kisses, or I should say my ecclesiastical cousin's salute belonged to one of these classes ..." (p.424).

A direct address to the reader is used to show the importance of Jane's continuous thoughts of Mr Rochester. The intensity of her feeling for him despite their separation is shown in powerful natural imagery, the thought of him "was not a vapour sunshine could disperse, nor a sand-traced effigy storms could wash away ..." (p.424). The disappointment at not receiving answers to her letters requesting news is described in similarly natural terms; as hope dies, it is like the feeble efforts of a spark in a dead fire, "it shone ... it faded, flickered ... died out ... dark indeed" (p.425). The contrast of her present relationship with St John and the passion of her feelings for Mr Rochester is clear as her responses to St John are almost like an automaton's, with no natural spontaneity: "I, like a fool, never thought of resisting him — I could not resist him" (p.425). He does not show any gentleness or fondness towards her; when she cries, he "expressed no surprise at this emotion ... he sat calm and patient, leaning on his desk ..." (p.425).

St John asks Jane to come to India as his wife, but in a most cold and calculating way. She has a difficult dilemma to resolve but is certain they cannot marry as they have different ideas of love. When he takes her out on to the moors, to ask her to come out as a fellow worker with him to India, the beauty of the English countryside is described to show what she would have to reject, and the claustrophobic atmosphere emphasises the stifling of her spirit which would inevitably take place if she agreed: "the hills, meantime, shut us quite in" (p.426); "I felt as if an awful charm was framing round and gathering over me" (p.427). The dramatic language of elaborate hymns is again used to show his exalted view of his vocation: "I am the servant of an infallible master ... my king, my lawgiver, my captain, is the all-perfect ... offer them, direct from God, a place in the ranks of his chosen" (p.427). In contrast, it is in natural terms that Jane describes the shock of realising his intentions: "The glen and sky spun round; the hills heaved!" (p.427). The most forceful evidence of the lack of emotional support in his suggestion, so necessary to someone of Jane's passionate nature, is in the demanding and imperious tone of his conclusion: "A missionary's wife you must — shall be. You shall be mine: I claim you — not for my pleasure, but for my Sovereign's service" (p.428). There is no hint that her pleasure has even been considered.

Despite Jane's protests, St John's calculating and cold attitude is made even clearer when he admits "I have watched you ever since we first met: I have made you my study for ten months" (p.428). She is described as an object in a scientific experiment, not as a human being. He is determined to interpret her actions to suit his purposes, not to recognise the natural generosity of spirit and childlike delight in her situation: "In the resolute readiness with which you cut your wealth into four shares ... I recognised a soul that revelled in the flame and excitement of sacrifice" (p.429). The imagery of claustrophobia and constriction is again used to suggest how this life in India as his assistant would crush and stifle her: "My iron shroud contracted round me ..." (p.429). St John's nature is like the cold hardness of iron, and the image of a shroud suggests that Jane's freer and more natural responses would die in his restrictive lifestyle.

The dilemma Jane is faced with is shown effectively in the flood of questions and arguments and counter-arguments she thinks through, trying to persuade herself that to accept would be the best course, even though she knows "he prizes me as a soldier would a good weapon, and that is all" (p.430). The determination with which she works out what is most abhorrent to her in his requests, the form of marriage with no love, and then decides to accept apart from that, shows her sense of duty once again denying her true desires. Her language is direct and clear to emphasise her resolution: "I am ready to go to India, if I may go free" (p.430). Jane's belief in, and previous experience of, true love, and St John's denial of it, emphasise their incompatibility. This is also shown in his rejection of the idea that they should go to India as brother and sister; marriage to him is merely a practical necessity, "... either our union must be consecrated by marriage, or it cannot exist: practical obstacles oppose themselves to any other plan" (p.430). His role as husband is clearly seen merely as possessor, as having within his control an instrument to aid his work, not a person to care for: "I want a wife: the sole helpmeet I can influence efficiently in life, and retain absolutely till death" (p.431).

Jane's spirited response to St John's suggestion that her devotion must be complete is shown in the admission of sarcasm in her reply: "'Oh! I will give my heart to God,' I said. *'You* do not want it'" (p.431). Her independence and sense of self-worth, frequently emphasised by the author as important to a woman in a world where men dominated, is shown in a very similar way to that when she was arguing with Mr Rochester: "I was an equal — one with whom I might argue — one whom, if I saw good, I might resist" (p.432). This is what gives her the courage to stand up against St John's religious persuasiveness; if she resisted marriage to him, "I should still have my unblighted self to turn to: my natural unenslaved feelings ... recesses in my mind which would be only mine ..." (p.433). Each is shown to be as obstinate as the other and Jane becomes even more admirable as she stands up to St John's assumption of superiority and shows him he cannot have his own way; challenging his lack of humanity in not being able to know real love, "I scorn the counterfeit sentiment you offer; yes, St John, and I scorn you when you offer it" (p.433).

St John's determination overcomes even this direct slight, despite Jane's pleading for him to see that they have totally differing ideas of love which can never be reconciled, as he still does not give up. He even resorts to emotional blackmail when asking her to consider her response while he is away in Cambridge: "... do not forget that if you reject it, it is not me you deny, but God" (p.434). This implies, as the author seemed to do earlier, that in fact he has a somewhat false notion of Christianity, adhering rigidly to duty and overlooking the quality of compassion. This seems further underlined when Jane goes after him to wish him goodnight: "... no cheering smile or generous word: but still the Christian was patient and placid ..." (p.435). The reference to the lack of kindness in connection with calling him Christian implies a challenge to the true nature of the clergyman's vocation, a suggestion that his spirituality is distancing him from its appropriate human expression.

Questions on Chapter Thirty-four

1. How does her new wealth affect Jane and the Rivers family?
2. How is the contrast of Jane's and St John's natures shown in this chapter?
3. How does the language used by the characters reflect their attitudes?
4. Where in this chapter does the author show her concern for women's independence?

Glossary

P.417 Sensual: physical
P.417 Affluence: wealth
P.418 Amenities: pleasant comforts
P.420 Exertion: activity
P.422 Robust: strong
P.427 Infallible: unfailing
P.429 Revelled: delighted

P.430 Consecrated: made holy, recognised by the church
P.433 Unblighted: unspoiled, uncorrupted
P.433 Recesses: depths
P.433 Counterfeit: false

Chapter Thirty-five

Summary

St John behaves in a very reserved and formal manner towards Jane and the coldness of his manner forces her to try to make friends and attempt to lighten the atmosphere. Diana sympathises with Jane's refusal to go to India and shows her understanding despite her disappointment that her brother and Jane will not be married. St John persists obstinately in his insistence on Jane becoming his wife, and she has almost been forced into accepting when she is diverted by believing she is called by Mr Rochester.

Commentary

St John behaves very coldly and the house is filled with an uneasy atmosphere. The tension in the house is well conveyed in the opening paragraphs of this chapter, with St John's brooding presence and his silent disapproval; Jane comments that in appropriate Christian duty he has forgiven her but "he had not forgotten the words; and as long as he and I lived he would never forget them" (p.436). This is another example of St John living by the letter but not the full spirit of his Christian principles; he is totally virtuous but not totally humane. His inhumanity is emphasised in the repetition of images previously used to suggest his cold, hard manner: "... no longer flesh, but marble; his eye was a cold, bright blue gem ..." (p.436).

The formal language St John uses in the conversation with Jane when she tries to renew their friendship and the "cool tranquil tone" (p.437) of his words, underlie this coldness even further and the appropriate image of an avalanche is used to suggest the overwhelming power of his displeasure, suggesting a death by freezing, as Jane feels she is experiencing: "If I were to marry you, you would kill me. You are killing me now" (p.438). The argument about going to India continues, as each will not move from their position; Jane is ready to go as an assistant but never as St John's wife; he will take her only as his wife. Jane's boldness and spirit is again indicated in her direct and challenging response to him: "You are not really shocked; for, with your superior mind, you cannot be either so dull or so conceited as to misunderstand my meaning ..." (p.439). Her own intelligence is evident here; to be able to recognise his nature, and to emphasise the qualities on which he must pride himself, is clearly perceptive and skilful.

St John's attitude to Jane's feeling for Mr Rochester is harsh and uncompromising, again showing how totally he has denied desire in himself as he insists in very formal terms: "The interest you cherish is lawless and unconsecrated. Long since you ought to have crushed it: now you should blush to allude to it" (p.439). His reference to an 'interest' and using 'it' rather than 'he' shows once again his lack of humanity and this is emphasised by the contrast with his sister, when Diana shows her concern and sympathy for Jane. Her desire for a marriage between her brother and Jane is quickly rejected when she hears the terms St John has made; this is shown in the swift transition from one exclamation, "That is just what we hoped and thought!", to another, "Madness! You would not live three months there ..." (p.440).

Diana sympathises with Jane's situation and Jane tries to explain exactly why she feels she and St John are so incompatible. A little lightness is introduced into the atmosphere through Diana's exaggerated horror at the likely effect of India on Jane: "You are much too pretty, as well as too good, to be grilled alive in Calcutta" (p.441). The sympathetic response helps Jane to explain, for herself as much as Diana, exactly why she and St John are incompatible, and this leads to an admirable summary of the inhumanity previously suggested: "He is a good and a great man; but he forgets, pitilessly, the feelings and claims of little people, in pursuing his own large views" (p.441). The dramatic reading of the Bible yet again enforces this view; he is totally absorbed in his own righteousness and in the condemnation of what he sees as weakness and sin in others: "... the second death.' Henceforward, I knew what fate St John feared for me ... The reader believed his name was already written in the Lamb's Book of Life ..." (p.442).

The amazing persistence and obstinacy of St John is also shown as he still seems to think Jane could change her mind about marriage; he is arrogantly describing himself in terms of Christ as he suggests: "If I listened to human pride, I should say no more to you of marriage with me; but I listen to my duty ... My Master was long-suffering: so will I be" (p.443). There is a very dramatic description of the mental and spiritual battle Jane is involved in; the vigorous language emphasises this: "... struggling ... rush down the torrent ... into the gulf ... hard beset ... wrestlings paralysed ... a sudden sweep ... life rolled together ..." (p.443-444). The writing is skilfully developed to increase the suspense as the reader wonders if Jane will succumb to St John's relentless insistence and emotional blackmail, culminating in the desperate plea, "Show me, show me the path!" and the haunting call, "Jane! Jane! Jane!" (p.444).

The contrast of the sonorous power of religious phrases from St John and the pitiful, pleading voice Jane believes to be that of Rochester's spirit, calling "in pain and woe, wildly, eerily, urgently" (p.445), is most effective, and Jane's response, after her first wild reaction in rushing outdoors, is equally a contrast, a natural response rather than the artificial extremity of religious intensity drawn from her by St John. She denies the power of witchcraft and insists, "it is the work of nature. She was roused, and did — no miracle — but her best" (p.445). The strength of her real feelings and her true self are sufficient to reject St John's power over her completely: "I desired him to leave me: I must and would be alone.

He obeyed at once" (p.p.445). The short, direct sentences also contrast effectively with the elaborate and exalted language of St John, underlining the victory achieved in denying his persuasions.

Questions on Chapter Thirty-five

1. How is St John's inhumanity illustrated in this chapter?
2. What details show Jane's perceptiveness and understanding?
3. What further evidence is there in this chapter of the theme of the struggle between duty and desire?

Glossary

P.35   Allude: refer

Chapter Thirty-six

Summary

Jane rushes away from Morton as soon as possible, explaining to the Rivers sisters that she has to find out about some friends. She goes back to Thornfield to find it a blackened ruin, after having been destroyed by fire. She returns to the inn where the coach had left her and inquires about the house from the landlord. He tells her that Bertha, the mad Mrs Rochester, had started the fire in the middle of one night and that she had fallen from the roof during the blaze and killed herself. Mr Rochester had been blinded and crippled as he had refused to leave the burning building before everyone else had got out. Jane learns where he is living and immediately arranges for a carriage to take her there to Mr Rochester.

Commentary

Jane leaves Morton and returns to Thornfield Hall, prompted by the voice of Mr Rochester which she thinks she had heard calling her. The dawn of the next day, which Jane waited for at the end of the previous chapter, is mentioned very abruptly, with a sense of foreboding, increased by the usual comparison with the weather: "the morning was overcast and chilly: rain beat fast on my casement" (p.446). St John's insistence does not let up even at this stage as a note is passed under Jane's door, expressing, in pompous language, concern for her soul: "watch and pray that you enter not into temptation ..." (p.446).

The power of the supernatural, a theme presented previously in terms of the mad Mrs Rochester, is introduced again in reference to the sense of Rochester calling to Jane. Through her character's meditations, the author presents the idea that perhaps such effects are in fact part of our unconscious selves, like dreams, revealing feelings pushed aside or rejected: "I questioned whence it came, as vainly as before: it seemed in *me* — not in the external world" (p.446).

The strength of feeling for Mr Rochester is clear in Jane's determination to find out what has happened to him: "I will know something of him whose voice seemed last night to summon me ... Once more on the road to Thornfield, I felt like the messenger-pigeon flying home" (p.447). The image suggests that her rightful place is with Rochester, that the year apart from him was some kind of test she forced on herself out of duty. The coincidence that it was exactly a year since she got down from the coach at the same spot, destitute and alone, emphasises a stage of life completed, another phase of the journey to self-knowledge accomplished.

Suspense is built up as Jane gets nearer and nearer to the house; then she is shocked to see it is in ruins and totally deserted. Jane's delight at being once again near Thornfield is dampened by her dutiful self challenging her desirous self; this is personified in her comment: "'You have lost your labour — you had better go no farther,' urged the monitor" (p.448). Her excitement overcomes her restraint, however, and this is shown in the frequent exclamations as she draws nearer Rochester's home: "How fast I walked! How I ran sometimes!" (p.448), and her happy response to a familiar landscape, seeing the natural surroundings personified as friends: "I welcomed single trees I knew ..." (p.448).

The gradual approach to the house is made suspenseful for the reader, at first, "I could peep round quietly", then, "I advanced my head ... A peep and then a long stare ... a sudden stop ... " (p.449). The suspense is increased even further with the 'illustration', preparing for the shock Jane experiences by referring to a lover finding his sweetheart dead; then the stark, abrupt, short sentence contrasts with the previous extended metaphor: "I looked with timorous joy towards a stately house; I saw a blackened ruin" (p.449). The eerie nature of the burnt-out house is emphasised by the reference back to the dream Jane once had of trying to protect a baby while stumbling through Thornfield Hall as just such "a dreary ruin" (p.310), before her intended marriage to Rochester. The desolation of the place is shown clearly in the lack of answers to Jane's almost frenzied questions: "there was no one here to answer it — not even dumb sign, mute token" (p.450).

Jane eventually learns from the landlord that Mr Rochester is now living at Ferndean and arranges to go to him at once. Jane's terror at the possibility that Mr Rochester is dead is effectively suggested when she returns to the inn and asks the landlord for the story of the house. He mentions the "late" Mr Rochester and Jane, in her agitated state of mind, immediately assumes the worst until reassured: "'I mean the present gentleman Mr Edward's father,' he explained" (p.450). The story is gradually told and the reader is involved in the discovery with the character, especially the chilling news that the fire which destroyed the house happened at the time when the mad Mrs Rochester had previously caused havoc and disturbance: "'At the dead of night!' I muttered. Yes, that was ever the hour of fatality at Thornfield" (p.451). The irony of the landlord talking of Jane, without realising he is actually talking to her, lightens the atmosphere a little: "... nobody but him thought her so very handsome. She was a little, small thing, they say, almost like a child" (p.451-452).

The story of the fire is told in detail, with a sense that the landlord enjoys the role of narrator. The destructive passion of Mrs Rochester is made clear when Jane is told she might well have been killed had she still been living in the house: "... made her way to the chamber that had been the governess's ... had a spite at her — and she kindled the bed there; but there was nobody sleeping in it, fortunately" (p.452). The drama of the tale increases as the landlord tells of the death of Mrs Rochester; she is described as devilish in her demented state, her long black hair "streaming against the flames as she stood ... she yelled and gave a spring, and the next minute she lay smashed on the pavement" (p.453).

Again suspense is introduced to the story as Jane gradually hears of Mr Rochester's situation: "Poor Mr Edward ... Some say it was a just judgement ... many think he had better be dead ... he can't get out of England ..." (p.453). At last the man tells her exactly what has happened to him: "He is stone-blind" (p.454); it is almost a relief as Jane had imagined so much worse, and knowledge of the heroic actions which led to his being blinded only increase her admiration and love for him; now she knows he is free, even though "blind, and a cripple" (p.454); she can go to him freely herself, no longer bound by duty to stay away because of the presence of a wife. Yet another place, Ferndean, is added to the list of those houses which have seen the development of Jane and the stages of her life, as she prepares to rush to the side of the man she can now openly love.

Questions on Chapter Thirty-six

1. How does the author keep the reader involved and interested in the story in this chapter?
2. How is Jane's need and love for Mr Rochester emphasised?
3. What is the effect of using the landlord of the inn as a narrator?

Glossary

P.451 Fatality: death

Chapter Thirty-seven

Summary

Jane reaches Rochester's new home and asks to be shown in to him without announcement. When he realises it is her, he can hardly believe she is not a supernatural creature conjured up by his desperate longing for her. She offers herself as his companion, privately hoping that he wants her as his wife. They are uncertain of each other, and only after long, teasing conversations and tantalising hesitations and uncertainties, does he eventually propose to her for the second time, and she accepts.

Commentary

Jane still admires and loves Rochester, more rather than less now he has lost his independence and is blind and crippled. She offers to be his companion. The retreating and hidden nature of Mr Rochester's life since the fire is made clear in the description of Ferndean as Jane approaches it: "deep buried in a wood ... so thick and dark grew the timber of the gloomy wood about it ... a grass-grown track ... stretched on and on ... dense summer foliage — no opening anywhere" (p.455). Jane's admiration of Mr Rochester is shown in her reaction to her first sight of him at Ferndean: "His form was of the same strong and stalwart contour as ever", but her sympathy and tenderness is also shown in her perceptive recognition that "reminded me of some wronged and fettered wild beast or bird" (p.456); she is instantly aware of his restless sense of confinement and dissatisfaction.

Jane's image of him is strong and masterful despite his handicaps; he is seen as "Samson", and an "eagle", implying power and grandeur (p.456); then the direct address involves the reader in the situation: "do you think I feared him in his blind ferocity?" (p.456) and suspense is again created as Jane does not immediately address him. The obstinate independence of Rochester is shown as Jane watches his attempts to walk around the grounds and his refusal of John's help; this is confirmed when she decides to stay overnight and asks to see him, as Mary responds: "he refuses everybody" (p.457). Jane's nervousness in approaching Rochester as she takes his drink and candle is shown in physical reactions: "the tray shook as I held it; the water split from the grass; my heart struck my ribs loud and fast" (p.457).

The frustration at his disability shown by Mr Rochester is poignant as he tries to work out who has come in: "Who is this? Who is this?' he demanded, trying, as it seemed, to *see* with those sightless eyes — unavailing and distressing attempt!" (p.458). His desperation is dramatically shown in his plea, "Whatever, whoever you are, be perceptible to the touch, or I cannot live!" (p.458). The simplicity of the final reunion is very moving; the straightforward language and direct sentences emphasise the tenderness between them far more effectively than elaborate imagery: "She is all here: her heart too' ... 'Jane Eyre! — Jane Eyre!' was all he said" (p.458).

Rochester is eager to learn of how Jane has lived since she left Thornfield and is jealous of the relationship with Rivers. The longing Rochester has experienced in his solitary life is emphasised in the contrast between his dreams of Jane, when he "felt that she loved me, and trusted that she would not leave me ... I always woke and found it an empty mockery" (p. 459), and the reality.

Jane's spirited self-reliance is underlined in her delight in being able to declare, "I am an independent woman now" (p.459). She had so longed not to be beholden to anyone; it is only in this new independence that she can come to Rochester in this way, knowing his wife is dead and that she can stay with him forever. As with her reaction to the inheritance when she heard of it from St John Rivers, it is the independence which the money brings her, rather than the materialistic love of money for itself, which so pleases her: "I told you I am independent, sir, as well as rich: I am my own mistress" (p.459).

At last Jane's sense of duty can be combined with her desires, as she declares to Rochester, "I will be your companion — to read to you, to walk with you, to sit with you, to wait on you, to be eyes and hands to you" (p.460). As before, neither of them is able to say directly how deeply they feel for each other, each assuming the other wants only companionable friendship rather than marriage; by this means the author makes the reader impatient and almost irritated by their hesitancy: "I suppose I should now entertain none but fatherly feelings for you ... I am content to be only your nurse, if you think it better" (p.460). Also as before, Jane is concerned not to let Rochester indulge in self-pity; this would diminish him in her admiration; when he asks if his disabilities make him revolting to her, she counters with the suggestion that "one is in danger of loving you too well for all this; and making too much of you" (p.461). Eventually a more comfortable mood is established: "I was at perfect ease, because I knew I suited him ... in his presence I thoroughly lived; and he lived in mine" (p.461).

The wonder and pleasure Rochester feels in Jane's presence is shown in his difficulty in believing she is really with him; he has longed for her so much he wonders if he is merely suffering from a delusion. This makes the situation more realistic; in contrast with the dull, hopeless mood he has been suffering, he is full of delight and amazement: "And the enchantment there is in the very hour I am now spending with you. Who can tell what a dark, dreary, hopeless life I have dragged on for months past?" (p.462). The reference to "enchantment" suggests he is still half wondering if she is a supernatural, rather than human, being. Jane's directness, which has always pleased Mr Rochester, is evident in her comments on his appearance, again refusing to indulge him in any way; the exchange is quite amusing: "'Am I hideous, Jane?' 'Very, sir; you always were, you know.'" (p.463).

Now he has her with him again, Rochester begins to feel jealous of possible friends she may have made while she has been away; this feeling is increased by her teasing of him, refusing to give details of the people she has been staying with, which in turn shows how comfortable she must feel with him now: "'Who have you been with, Jane?' 'You shall not get it out of me to-night ...' 'Were there only ladies in the house where you have been?' I laughed and made my escape ..." (p.463).

The next morning Jane's compassion for Rochester is shown in the imagery used to describe his blind dependence, as if the light of his spirit has been dulled: "His countenance reminded one of the lamp quenched, waiting to be re-lit" (p.464). The natural light, in contrast, is shown to be a reflection of happier days to come and a joyous mood, "The rain is over and gone, and there is a tender shining after it" (p.464). Again, natural imagery is used to emphasise the poignancy of a strong, forceful man rendered ineffectual by his disability: "just as if a royal eagle, chained to a perch, should be forced to entreat a sparrow to become its purveyor" (p.464). Jane's typical concern for others rather than herself is shown here and also in her account of her past year as "I softened considerably what related to the three days of wandering and starvation, because to have told him all would have been to inflict unnecessary pain" (p.464-465).

The jealousy already shown in Rochester is immediately re-awakened at the mention of St John Rivers in Jane's account; it is amusing as he clearly wants to find faults in the other man: "Is he a person of low stature ... his brain? That is probably rather soft? ... His manners, I think you said, are not to your taste?" (p.465). The eagerness with which Rochester suggests these defects clearly shows how concerned he is that Jane might prefer being with St John to being with him. The image of the snake, previously used when

Jane was testing out Rochester's feelings at Thornfield, is appropriate again: "Jealousy had got hold of him: she stung him; but the sting was salutary ... I would not, therefore, immediately charm the snake" (p.466). As always, Jane is aware of what would be best for Rochester, how he ought to behave, how he should be encouraged to respond.

Jane's sense of propriety forces her to resist immediately showing her true desire for Rochester; she teases him when he appeals for flattery but eventually accepts his second proposal of marriage. Her moral code imposes an amusing attitude towards him, as if she is his governess; she is probably enjoying a measure of power over him, as the author probably enjoyed depicting this. The same hint of superiority is shown in her teasing him again, not flattering him as he might have wished, in response to another remark about his appearance: "you certainly are rather like Vulcan, sir" (p.466). His remark about the mythical blacksmith, traditionally seen as a thickset, swarthy character, clearly does fit him well, but Jane's immediate confirmation of this does not allow for any gentle encouragement; she is as direct and firm as ever. The conversation between them about her stay at Morton is continued and the short, sharp exchanges (p.467) show the tension between them and his agitation about her life away from him. The mention of the Hindustani becomes almost ridiculous, as Jane does not attempt to explain in detail at once, but only answers exactly what he asks her, almost like a little game she is playing with him: "'Did you ask to learn?' 'No.' 'He wished to teach you?' 'Yes.'" (p.467).

When she admits St John asked her to marry him, the circumstances have become so much like a game that Rochester thinks this "... is also teasing, " ... an impudent invention to vex me" (p.467). She eventually admits that although she had been asked to marry Rivers, she was teasing him over the situation: "Oh, you need not be jealous! I wanted to tease you a little to make you less sad: I thought anger would be better than grief" (p.468). At last she directly declares her true feelings: "All my heart is yours, sir: it belongs to you; and with you it would remain, were fate to exile the rest of me from your presence for ever" (p.469). Rochester uses natural imagery to complement that used by Jane of the bird, describing himself and her in terms of the old tree and youthful plant, "what right would that ruin have to bid a budding woodbine cover its decay with freshness?" (p.469). When at last he asks her to marry him, it is only after more verbal sparring, she suggesting she had no idea she knew he even wanted a wife, let alone herself. Eventually, however however, his second proposal to her and its acceptance is in very simple, direct language, with no more hinting and hesitating.

The rightness of Jane's decision in accepting Rochester is shown in the religious terms Rochester uses, demonstrating how different this acceptance is to the potential acceptance of Rivers, even though in the same kind of terms: "What do I sacrifice? Famine for food, expectation for content ... certainly I delight in sacrifice" (p.470). The kind of sacrifice she would have made as St John's wife would have destroyed her; this kind of sacrifice will only enhance her happiness and well-being. Rochester shows the same eagerness to marry quickly as he did before, but this time for eagerness to be with the one he loves, rather than in order to avoid any challenge to the match. Again, the religious quality of the language is strong as he tells of his desperation for Jane's comforting presence, but this time the language is direct and sincere, rather than pompous and distant, as St John's was: "I supplicated God, that, if it seemed good to him, I might soon be taken from this life, and admitted to that world to come, where there was still hope of joining Jane" (p.471).

The supernatural link between Rochester and Jane is finally confirmed in the matching up of his call to her and her answer to him; the author suggests that the natural bond between them was so strong that no human situation or circumstance could eventually stop their union: "In spirit, I believe, we must have met" (p.472).

Jane's superstitious response to this shows her natural caution, denying the truth of positive events to avoid possible disappointment, as she had done previously: "The coincidence struck me as too awful and inexplicable to be communicated or discussed" (p.472). The final image of this chapter, of Jane as "his prop and guide" (p.473), is most satisfying after the various hesitations and uncertainties before they could be sure of each other again. This realistic element, as well as being tantalising to the reader, makes the story much more believable.

Questions on Chapter Thirty-seven

1. How does the author keep the reader in suspense during several parts of this chapter?
2. What different aspects of Jane's personality and temperament are shown in this chapter?
3. How is the natural imagery used to good effect here?
4. How is the drama of this stage of the story shown?

Glossary

P.456 Ferocity: fierceness
P.458 Unavailing: fruitless, failing
P.464 Purveyor: provider
P.467 Impudent: cheeky
P.467 Vex: anger

Chapter Thirty-eight

Summary

Jane and Rochester are married; their life together is described and events in other characters' lives are summarised, as if the final chapter is written from the viewpoint of several years later. Jane has a son and Rochester recovers his sight.

Commentary

Jane describes the quick, quiet marriage arrangement, the servants' reactions and the happy life she leads with Rochester. The direct, short opening sentence is important as it makes Jane the dominant partner: "I married him", rather than "He married me". She is now the leader in life literally and metaphorically, owing to his disability and her financial independence. She has always been shown to be of independent spirit, but here the author shows that the full independence, constantly striven for, has been achieved. Jane seems very matter-of-fact about the whole arrangement; it is certainly seen as more of an arrangement than a ceremony: "Mary, I have been married to Mr Rochester this morning" (p.474), and Jane is glad not to have any fuss made about it, no "torrent of wordy wonderment" (p.474), expressed.

The description of the servants' reaction, though subdued, is quite amusing, "the ladle ... did for some three minutes hang suspended in air, and for the same space of time John's knives also had rest from the polishing process" (p.474). It is as if the implements had lives of their own and were not held in human hands; the gap of time, although very short, suggests a state of suspended animation, to express delight and surprise.

Mr Rochester at last feels confident enough to express unreserved tenderness when he talks of their honeymoon lasting the rest of their lives: "its beams will only fade over your grave or mine" (p.475). The author ties up loose ends in this final chapter by using the method of direct address from the character: Jane reports the communication with St John and then recalls Adele, almost seen as a substitute child by Jane, though she cannot care for her at home, "I took care she should never want for anything that could contribute to her comfort" (p.475). Clearly the last chapter is meant to be commenting on events from some years ahead in time as Jane remarks, "By her grateful attention to me and mine, she has long since well repaid any little kindness" (p.475). The prejudice against foreign manners is quite amusingly implied in the comment, "a sound English education corrected in great measure her French defects" (p.475).

The independence her relationship has given her is again shown to be the most treasured aspect of her final phase of life as recounted in the novel, as she says, "I am my husband's life as fully as he is mine ... to be together is for us to be at once as free as solitude, as gay as in company" (pp.475-476). This suggests that the situation is the author's idea of a perfect relationship, showing a concern for women's needs and desires to be respected at a time when they were nearly always seen as merely the property of their husbands; their purpose to keep them happy, rather than achieving mutual content, as Jane and Rochester do, "he felt I loved him so fondly, that to yield that attendance was to indulge my sweetest wishes" (p.476).

Final details of other characters' lives are given so that the reader can see the full picture. The fullness of the relationship is completed with the birth of their child and the partial recovery of Mr Rochester's sight; the author ends with something of the traditional happy ending but much more realistically than in many novels written at the time. The happy marriages of the Rivers sisters reflect their positive and caring natures, and the continuing friendship of the three families gives the reader an idea of a continuing framework for the lives of characters beyond the novel, making them more realistic and believable.

Rochester expresses the underlying Christian values of the novel in Jane's recollection of his remark: "God had tempered judgement with mercy" (p.477). The contrasting harshness and rigidity of the extreme Christian viewpoint of St John Rivers ends the novel, in terms of respect, but also suggesting that Jane and the author felt truer, more natural happiness was gained in the moderation of human kindness and sympathy. He has clearly worn himself out in his relentless pursuit of virtue: "A more resolute, indefatigable pioneer never wrought amidst rocks and dangers" (p.477). Clearly, the final reference to his longing for death and the afterlife is shown to be an indication that Jane would also have been worn out as his companion, and that her happiness is well deserved; she can continue to show Christian kindness and compassion to her family and friends.

Questions on Chapter Thirty-eight

1. In what different ways does the author show the happiness Jane and Rochester at last achieve?
2. How is Jane shown to have attained full independence and maturity at the end of the novel?
3. What details of other characters' lives tie up loose ends in this final chapter?

Glossary

P.477 Tempered: moderated
P.477 Indefatigable: untirable

PART TWO

Themes and Sample Questions & Answers

Answering Questions Involving Themes

Now that you have read the whole novel and know the story and characters quite well, you need to think about the way in which you are expected to show this knowledge in answering examination questions. A very important thing to remember is that you **cannot** show all you know, nor should you merely tell the story in your own words. You need to take particular note of the actual words of the question and concentrate on that specific aspect of the text.

A good way of practising this is to consider the major **themes** of the novel — the ideas and topics which are explored throughout the text, gradually developing more and more significance as the story develops. While reading through this study guide, you will have noticed that in the commentaries there are a number of themes which are frequently referred to and recalled. The most important of these are:

i.   Education

We can see the whole novel as an example of a story of the development and maturing of a central character. Also, this theme is explored in terms of the author's interest in different types of education and schooling and their effects on those taught.

ii.   Women's independence

In our own time we can see what might be called a feminist perspective in the novel; Charlotte Bronte may not have expressed it quite like that, but she was certainly aware of the need for greater recognition of women's writing, having had to publish initially under a male pseudonym.

iii.   The natural world and its reflection of human situations

The very frequent use of natural imagery is constantly referred to in the commentaries — this is a particular feature of the author's style and would be relevant in most answers to exam questions.

iv. The power of the supernatural and importance of dreams

This, as with (iii) above, is a typical feature of the romantic style which Charlotte Bronte was developing and extending in her work. Supernatural events are not only negative — Helen Burns' view of God and Heaven are supernatural as much as Jane's terrible hallucination in the red-room.

v. Religion and morality

Charlotte Bronte clearly adheres to a traditional Christian ethic, but she challenges excessively rigid interpretation of this. She strongly implies that humanity and natural human compassion are more important than strict observance of a creed.

In order to prepare to answer a question on such areas, you need to work through the novel with the commentaries to help you and locate all references to the particular theme. Then you will need to select those references which you feel are most important, as in a timed examination you will not have time to include them all. Once you have made a selection, you need to relate the references to the exact words of the question. The following examples should help you to apply the same technique to each theme; this will be an excellent method of revision of the text.

Sample Questions and References from the Text

i. Education

a. How important do you feel the theme of education is to the novel as a whole?

b. To what extent is *Jane Eyre* a novel exploring the development and maturity of an individual?

c. How is the author's interest in education and schooling reflected in the experiences of the central character?

d. How far do the different places where Jane lives and works represent stages in her development and understanding?

1. *Chapter 1 p.39:* When Jane is living in the Reed household, the importance of books as an escape is introduced. The education theme is involved as Jane is learning to rely on her own resources, to retreat from unkindness and teasing.

2. *Chapter 4:* In this chapter the idea of Jane going to school is developed; Mr Brocklehurst, the headmaster of Lowood, is introduced; the author is giving a clear insight into the harshness of institutional schooling such as she and her sisters endured for some time at Cowan Bridge.

3. *Chapter 4 p.69:* Jane's development as a character is shown in her outburst against her aunt's unfair treatment.

4. *Chapter 5:* More details of Lowood life; p. 81: Jane notices that the school is referred to as an institution; the lessons are very much instruction rather than exploration of the subjects studied.

5. *Chapter 6:* More details of dull, monotonous lessons; p.87: further reference to the importance of books for escape from harsh reality; p.88 — 89: Miss Temple and Miss Scatcherd are contrasted; the difference in teaching methods emphasises the author's belief that it is much more satisfying to learn through interest than by rote.

6. *Chapter 7:* More detailed description of the treatment and lifestyle of Lowood pupils.

7. *Chapter 8:* Jane learns through the example of Helen Burns; p.106: the spiritual and intellectual nourishment of art is suggested.

8. *Chapter 10 p.121:* Jane's trunk represents stages in her life.

9. *Chapter 11:* Jane's approach to educating Adele is described through various comments.

10. *Chapter 13 p.153:* Jane's concern for her pupil's welfare shows her high standards as a governess.

11. *Chapter 15 p.177:* Jane's own education is developed through the stimulation and challenge of conversation with Mr Rochester.

12. *Chapter 17 p.205:* Comments about governesses reflect the low status of their role in society — the author's reaction is shown through Jane's bitter observations.

13. *Chapter 21 p.256:* Jane's personal development and maturity is shown in her reaction to her aunt when she dies — she recognises the ability to rise above childhood trauma in adulthood; p.268: Jane has learned from the example of her childhood friend, Helen Burns, as she offers her aunt the chance of reconciliation, in a spirit of forgiveness.

14. *Chapter 23 p.281:* Jane's own education through her conversations with Mr Rochester results in her love for him being partly founded in intellectual stimulation.

15. *Chapter 30 p.377:* Jane really enjoys the chance to be taught as well as teach in the company of the Rivers sisters. The pleasure in education and its benefits are clearly suggested here. P.381: when St John Rivers eventually suggests the position of schoolmistress to Jane, he implies it is a position very low in status; the author's concern that teaching should be more highly valued is hinted at when Jane delights in the possibility of the independence such a job would bring her.

16. *Chapter 32:* Jane's growing contentment and sense of achievement in her position of village schoolmistress shows the importance of education to both those who are taught and those who teach.

17. *Chapter 34:* More comments on the happiness and satisfaction gained through Jane's work as a teacher.

As previously suggested, you cannot hope to use all the references you find, especially if you have to remember them if you cannot take your text in to the examination. Therefore you need to try to group all the references and then pick one or two from each group to learn and use. Again the following example on the theme of Education should help you to follow the same procedure with the other themes suggested.

There are four main types of references:
a. References 1 and 5: the importance of books in providing another world to which to retreat;
b. References 1, 3, 7, 8, 11, 13 and 14: Jane's own development, learning from example, through growing maturity and the influence of others;
c. References 2, 4, 5, 6, 9 and 10: types of schooling, Jane's reaction to them and her own practice — reflecting the author's own attitudes or experience in most cases.
d. References 12, 15, 16 and 17: attitudes of others to education, particularly negative attitudes towards those who teach in terms of social status.

Let us look at question (a) on p. 201 : *How important do you feel the theme of education is to the novel as a whole?* In answering the question, you might explain, with a couple of the examples from each group of references, how these events in the novel contribute to the development of the story and make the characters realistic, remembering to **make it clear at each point** how you feel the example shows education to be important to the novel. You should be able to read back over your essay and look at any paragraph and know what the question was without looking at it - a sure test to see if you have really answered the question rather than just written vaguely about the text, or written vaguely about education, without connecting the two directly. Remember the examiner only knows what you mean if you write it; you cannot gain marks for intentions!

Having read over this example, now try to relate each group of references to questions (b) — (d) on education — the same material is relevant but you need to present it with different emphasis according to the question.

When you have practised on the Education theme, try to go through the other four main themes suggested, picking out the references, then grouping them, then applying them to the terms of the questions which follow:

ii. Women's independence

a. To what extent do you feel Charlotte Bronte could be presenting a feminist perspective in *Jane Eyre?*

b. Trace the personal development towards independence made by Jane in the novel.

c. Which two or three incidents in the novel most effectively indicate the author's concern for recognition of women's right to respect and personal freedom?

d. Where do you feel Jane most successfully expresses her spirited determination and self-reliance?

iii. The natural world and its reflection of human situations

a. To what effect does Charlotte Bronte use natural imagery in *Jane Eyre?*

b. Choose two or three incidents in the novel and show how the use of natural description enhances the presentation of character and setting.

c. How effectively do you feel the natural surroundings described in *Jane Eyre* reflect the feelings and situations experienced by the characters?

d. Choose one frightening incident, one happy incident and one sad incident in the story. How does the author link the natural world with the events in each case?

iv. The power of the supernatural and the importance of dreams

a. Consider three dreams in the story. Why are they important? How does the author create an emotional effect in connection with the dreams? How do the dreams relate to the progress of the novel and the development of the central character?

b. Illustrate the importance of the supernatural in *Jane Eyre*.

c. How does Charlotte Bronte prepare the reader for the supernatural events in the novel? Do you find that they make the text more or less realistic?

d. How do the dreams and supernatural events in *Jane Eyre* contribute to the mysterious element of the novel?

v. Religion and morality

a. Does the author suggest that there is a distinction between religion and morality in the novel?

b. Which characters in the novel could be described as particularly religious? How is this aspect of their character shown? Does their religious nature make them better people?

c. How does the central character, Jane Eyre, seem to view religion and morality? To what extent does her attitude change as she grows up?

d. Some of the concepts and ideas expressed by Helen Burns and St John Rivers are similar. How does the author show the similarities and differences between them in terms of their religious faith?

e. *Jane Eyre* was described by a contemporary reviewer as "an insult to piety". Discuss your view of Charlotte Bronte's treatment of religion and morality in the novel.

Context Questions

This is another kind of question you may be asked in an examination. Part of the text will be presented and you will be required to answer detailed questions on the style and content of the passage, and to relate it to the rest of the novel.

Throughout this study guide, the commentaries have been doing exactly this kind of work. Although no specific questions were answered, each of the points made on content and style could have been the answer to questions about such details. Thus a very good way of preparing for this kind of question is to use the commentaries on particularly important parts of the novel to help you think about what kind of questions you might be asked and how to answer them. The following example should help you to understand this method and to follow through other examples for yourself.

Look back at the very first page of the novel and the commentary on it. You could imagine that this page, apart from the last paragraph which is not complete on the page, was set as a context passage. It would start with "There was no possibility ..." and go on to "shrined in double retirement". You could use each of the points made in the commentary as answers to questions.

The first question might be literally to do with the context, i.e. where the passage occurs in the novel. You would hopefully recognise the context, but as it would be written out on the paper, there would be no direct indication that it was the start of the story. You would need to explain this, as one of the first points in the commentary refers to the novel opening right "in the middle of things", as if the reader already knows the characters and situation.

Following this method through, it is possible to imagine the following questions and answers:

i.   *At what point in the novel does the passage occur?*
     The passage occurs at the very beginning of the novel.

ii. *What is unusual about the first sentences? What effect do they create?*

The first sentences are unusual as the author starts straight into the story without introducing the various characters directly, as if the reader already knows who and where they are. This makes the readers bewildered, but also involves them immediately in the circumstances and encourages them to read further to find out who is who.

iii. *What kind of atmosphere is created in the first paragraph of the passage, and how?*

The atmosphere is grim and dark, suggested by the references to "the leafless shrubbery"; the "cold winter wind" and "sombre" clouds and "penetrating rain". (As in the commentaries, put any words you take directly from the passage into inverted commas, or speech marks. This is the best way of showing exactly what you mean, and that you have taken detailed notice of the set passage.)

iv. *Through whom does the author tell the story at this point? What is the narrator's situation?*

The author tells the story through Jane Eyre, the central character in the novel. She is living at Gateshead, the home of the Reed family, her aunt and cousins. She is in a difficult and unpleasant situation. The remarks about the usual "saddened" feeling after being told off by the nurse and the insecurity in being "humbled" by a sense of "inferiority" introduce a contrast between the narrator and the other characters mentioned: "Eliza, John and Georgina Reed". (It is not enough just to say she is in an unpleasant situation; you need to explain how the author shows this, by detailed comment on the text.)

v. *What impression is given of the Reed children and their mother in this passage?*

The Reed children seem very spoilt; they are "clustered" round their mother, as if to keep anyone else out of the comfortable circle; they seem discontented in their behaviour, "quarrelling" and "crying", but they are also deceitful as they appear "contented, happy little children" to their mother. She indulges them and refuses to see anything wrong in them. She treats them much better than Jane. She is harsh and unkind to Jane, assuming that she has done wrong and not allowing her to defend herself from unjust accusations, "... there is something truly forbidding in a child taking up her elders in that manner ...".

vi. *What does the reader learn of the central character in this passage?*

The reader learns that the central character is used to ill-treatment and has become resigned to it. She does not protest but shuts herself away from trouble. She finds comfort in books through which she can escape to another world.

In some context questions the marks for each question are printed on the paper. If this is so, if there are many more marks for some questions than others, obviously it is worth writing more for those which will gain most marks.

You could practise for this kind of question by approaching other key passages in the same way, for instance the description of the death of Helen Burns; the meeting with Mr Rochester on the road; the visitation of Bertha Moore in the night; the return to Gateshead and death of Mrs Reed; the dramatic stopping of the wedding; Jane's terrible journey across the moors; the contentment of her setting up school; the return to Rochester after the fire. There are many other incidents which you could consider, but all the passages listed above are very important parts of the story. In most cases, it would be unlikely that the passage for the context question would be more than the length of one page — as you can see, there is plenty to say about that length of text.